Cambridge Monographs on the History of Medicine

EDITORS: CHARLES WEBSTER AND CHARLES ROSENBERG

The Renaissance Notion of Woman

For Kirstie and Ewen

The Renaissance Notion of Woman

A STUDY IN THE FORTUNES OF SCHOLASTICISM AND
MEDICAL SCIENCE IN EUROPEAN
INTELLECTUAL LIFE

Ian Maclean

FELLOW OF THE QUEEN'S COLLEGE, OXFORD

The right of the
University of Cambridge
to print and sell
all manner of books
was granted by
Henry VIII in 1534.
The University has printed
and published continuously
since 1584.

CAMBRIDGE UNIVERSITY PRESS

CAMBRIDGE

NEW YORK   PORT CHESTER

MELBOURNE   SYDNEY

Published by the Press Syndicate of the University of Cambridge
The Pitt Building, Trumpington Street, Cambridge CB2 1RP
40 West 20th Street, New York, NY 10011, USA
10 Stamford Road, Oakleigh, Melbourne 3166, Australia

First published 1980
First paperback edition 1983
Reprinted 1985, 1988, 1990

Printed in Great Britain at the University Press, Cambridge

Library of Congress Cataloguing in Publication Data

Maclean, Ian, 1945–
The Renaissance notion of woman.
Includes bibliographical references and index.
1. Women – History – Renaissance, 1450–1600.
2. Europe – Intellectual life – History. I. Title.
HQ1148.M23   301.41'2'094   79–52837

ISBN 0 521 22906 5 hard covers
ISBN 0 521 27436 2 paperback

CONTENTS

PREFACE

The names of Renaissance writers are given where possible in their
vernacular form, except in cases where the Latin form is better known or
used in library catalogues (e.g. Cornelius a Lapide, Justus Lipsius). For
less well-known figures, the dates of birth and death, where known,
have been given, and the date of the earliest recorded edition of their
works which I could find. The major authorities consulted for this
information have been Zedler's *Universallexikon*, Hirsch's *Biographisches
Lexikon der hervorragenden Ärzte*, Cosenza's *Biographical and bibliographical dictionary of the Italian humanists*, R. J. Durling's *Catalogue of
sixteenth-century printed books in the National Library of Medicine*, *The
Oxford dictionary of the Christian Church*, ed. Cross and Livingstone, and
C. H. Lohr's alphabetical list of Renaissance Latin Aristotle commentaries (*Studies in the Renaissance*, XXI (1974), 228–89; *Renaissance
Quarterly*, XXVIII (1975), 689–741; XXIX (1976), 714–45; XXX (1977),
681–741). The first two authorities mentioned here are not wholly
reliable, and the dates have been included more to indicate the
approximate period of composition and publication of a text than in the
belief that they are well established. I have occasionally used standard
abbreviations (e.g. *PL* = *Patrologiae cursus completus, series latina*, ed. J. P.
Migne, Paris, 1844–1904; *PG* = *Patrologiae cursus completus, series graeca*,
ed. Migne, Paris, 1857–1904). In the case of long quotations, the original
text is given in the appendix; the original text of short quotations is
given in the endnotes. Translations from Aristotle are taken from *The
Works of Aristotle translated into English*, ed. W. D. Ross and J. A. Smith,
12 vols., Oxford, 1908–13. Paragraphs are numbered so that reference
can be made not only to individual ideas but also to the general context
of argument in which they are placed.

It would be impossible to acknowledge here the many debts which I
owe to scholars, but I should like to thank my colleagues at Queen's for
answering many fastidious questions; Charles Webster and Charles

Schmitt for making available to me the fruits of their wide erudition; the Queen's College, and the University of Oxford for generous grants to undertake research in London and Paris; the Institut Francophone in Paris for its academic hospitality; and my wife Pauline for her unfailing patience and her assistance with the preparation of the manuscript.

Oxford, October 1978

1

Introduction

1.1.1   A comprehensive modern history of woman in Renaissance
Europe has yet to be written. No doubt, when it appears it will show the
evolution of woman's place in society and relate this to suitable models –
demographic, anthropological, economic, sociological. Such a study
will draw on data from a wide variety of sources, and make use of the
information and conclusions of numerous monographs and theses. The
present study aspires only to survey a narrow band of the spectrum
which such a comprehensive history would need to cover; it does not set
out to answer questions about society or demography, but is limited to
the sphere of scholarship and scholarly texts. It is intended as a modest
contribution not only to the study of attitudes towards woman in the
Renaissance, but also to that of its intellectual infrastructure. It attempts
to offer tentative answers to the questions: what is the notion of woman
to be found in Renaissance texts, and how does it evolve?* What is the
relationship between the notion of woman and that of sex difference,
and how is sex difference related in turn to other differences? Two
presuppositions underlie these questions. The first is that there is less
change in the notion of woman throughout the Renaissance than
intellectual ferment and empirical enquiry of various kinds might lead
one to expect. The second is that, at the end of the Renaissance, there is a
greater discrepancy between social realities and the current notion of
woman than at the beginning. These presuppositions emerged from my
investigations into feminist writing in France in the first half of the
seventeenth century;[1] there seemed to be at that period both a survival
of a coherent scholastic notion of woman and an awareness on the part of

---

* The word 'notion' has been used here not to suggest an inflexible conceptual structure, but
rather a range of concepts (e.g. humanity, femaleness, femininity, difference), linked by more or less
definable relations (e.g. metaphysical, physical, social), which are subject to modification and
realignment within the general structure of 'notion'. Cf. L. J. Cohen's category of 'culture word',
The diversity of meaning, London, 1966, pp. 20ff.

scholars working in various fields that it was ill-justified by the evidence, and full of implicit inconsistencies. Such a development seemed to me to be worthy of further and wider study.

1.1.2   The limits of this wider study require some comment. It is generally accepted that after the establishment of printing as a means of disseminating texts, and before the development of strong vernacular and national intellectual traditions, there was a 'universe of discourse' expressed principally in Latin (but including also texts translated into various vernacular languages), which possessed common assumptions about academic disciplines. The temporal limits of this universe are not easily set, but they include the sixteenth century and the early part of the seventeenth. Its geographical boundaries encompass all European countries which received books published on matters of common academic interest, and perhaps also produced them: principally Italy, France, Germany, Spain, Great Britain and the Low Countries. Common academic interests include theology, medicine, law and 'practical philosophy' (ethics and politics), which are investigated in separate chapters in this study. All possess authoritative texts which attract commentary; this is not the case with ancient poetry and imaginative literature, another shared intellectual interest, and for this reason there is no separate examination of it here.

1.1.3   Inside these frontiers of time, place and intellectual discipline, there are three broad areas of enquiry to be pursued: the notion of woman itself; the idea of sex difference; the relationship between sex difference and other differences. From the earliest times, and in the most far-flung cultures, the notion of female has in some sense been opposed to that of male, and aligned with other opposites. The ways in which these opposites have been used in argumentation and related to each other are the subject of an illuminating investigation by G. E. R. Lloyd entitled *Polarity and analogy: two types of argumentation in early Greek thought* (Cambridge, 1971). The earliest stage in the use of polarity, in Lloyd's analysis, is represented by the related opposites attributed by Aristotle to the Pythagoreans in *Metaphysics* A.3 [986a 21ff]:

male	female
limit	unlimited
odd	even
one	plurality
right	left
square	oblong
at rest	moving

straight   curved
light   darkness
good   evil

Here there is no classification of the different sorts of opposites; nor is the alignment of male–limit–odd–one–right etc. justified by reasoning or empirical evidence. In the Renaissance, this set of opposites was known not only through Aristotle's account of it,[2] but also through the Hippocratic corpus, in which it is implicit.

1.1.4   Lloyd turns next to the use made of opposites by Eleatic philosophers, which is not relevant to this study; after this he considers Plato, whose interest in this topic is most clearly represented in the Renaissance by the theory of division, developed and resurrected principally by Ramus whose dichotomies are present in many texts of the late sixteenth and early seventeenth centuries.[3] Finally Lloyd examines Aristotle's own work, in which a more sophisticated analysis of these opposites and of modes of opposition is to be found, known to scholastic and Renaissance scholars alike.[4] Even in Jacopo Zabarella's innovative works on logic, this analysis is simply reproduced.[5] Its principal source is *Categories* x [11*b* 15ff]; there, opposites are divided into (1) correlative opposites (Zabarella's 'species relativa': e.g. double/half, father/son); (2) contraries, which can either admit an intermediate ('species contraria mediata': e.g. black/white) or not ('species contraria immediata': e.g. odd/even, health/sickness); (3) positive and privative terms ('species privata': e.g. sight/blindness); finally (4) contradictories ('species contradictoria': e.g. 'he sits'/'he does not sit'). The opposite male/female which is our concern here is sometimes an opposite of privation (see below, 2.2.1, 3.3.3), sometimes a contrary either admitting or not admitting an intermediate (see below, 3.5.5, 4.4.2, 5.3.1); it can attract parallels with correlative opposites (see below, 2.2.1, 4.4.3, 4.5.2). The complexity of the notion of woman, and the dislocations which occur within that notion, arise in part, as will be seen, from the structures of thought inherited from Aristotle.

1.1.5   The problem is exacerbated by the presence in intellectual life of unexplained and unjustified Pythagorean related dualities, not only in ancient medical texts, but also in the works of Aristotle himself, who treats the opposites right/left, above/below, front/back in this primitive manner, as Lloyd has shown.[6] The notion of the historical development of thought – either applied to earlier and later texts of the Aristotelian corpus, or to the relationship between this and the earlier Hippocratic corpus – is not invoked by Renaissance thinkers to resolve this confusion, and it seems that concepts of difference, division, definition and opposition are problematic to them. The notion of woman, intimately involved with this area of speculation, reflects well the hesitancies and incoherences inherent in Renaissance modes of thought.

1.2.1   It would be wrong to suggest, however, that humanist activity and scientific enquiry are alone the causes of change in the notion of woman. These arise also from political, social and economic factors extraneous to intellectual life. The question of society's influence on thought is vexed, but it cannot be disregarded altogether if the causes of change are to be investigated. Nor can those causes alone be considered of which contemporaries are themselves aware. On the other hand, the world of academic debate is to some degree protected from these outside influences; this is even more true of commentaries on and expositions of authoritative texts – the Bible, Aristotle, Galen, and so on – where the limits of the text in question help in turn to define and circumscribe the area of debate. The interpretation and discussion of authoritative texts takes place in commentary form throughout the Renaissance; specific passages which treat of woman will be examined here in order to assess the modification of views, if any, which takes place during this period.

1.2.2   Much is said about woman in the disciplines investigated in this book; but some parts of that discourse are privileged, and are taken as authoritative statements of their source. These are commonplaces (τόποι, *loci communes*).[7] They are used as vehicles to transmit conclusions and opinions from one discipline to another. The frequency of their quotation suggests that, for the Renaissance at least, intellectual disciplines were not remote from each other. Commentaries are not practised according to an identical method in all disciplines, but they all share the common functions of elucidation and cross-reference, both within and outside the particular text in question. This common function has been linked to an inherently religious and exegetic spirit in which language is assumed to have the objective status of a natural sign; this spirit is said to give way to a profane and critical attitude, emerging in the latter part of the seventeenth century, in which the text becomes not an object to be interpreted, repeated, preserved and exposed, but rather an actively organized means of designation whose language is functional and utilitarian.[8] The decline of commentary can therefore be linked with the rise of mechanism and functionalism (see below, 6.2.4). But commentary also embodies an educational or instructive purpose, whose means of expression varies in the Renaissance. Vulgarization by the use of vernacular paraphrases or dialogues, diagrammatic expositions after the manner of Ramus, dual-language (Greek and Latin) texts, commentaries by more than one hand are manifestations of different pedagogical needs and aims.

1.2.3   Renaissance scholars are aware of the existence of a stock of commonplaces about woman, and it is not rare to find pluridisciplinary accounts of her. Two examples of this may be briefly referred to here. The first is found in the French jurist André Tiraqueau's treatise on marriage law entitled *De legibus connubialibus*, which first appeared in 1513. It consists in later editions of over fifty folio pages of references to theology, medicine, ethics and ancient literature as well as law, in which a plethora of authorities establishes woman's inferiority to man. It represents one of the greatest collections of commonplaces about the female sex produced in the Renaissance. A second example is found in Book 3 of Baldassare Castiglione's *Il cortegiano* (1528), where, in dialogue form, the case for and against female inferiority is reproduced. Both examples demonstrate the use of authority and the currency of commonplaces; both reproduce synthetic views of woman which concord with the intellectual outlook of their day. By the end of the sixteenth century, however, some authorities have been questioned, some assumptions changed, some intellectual positions abandoned. It is the purpose of this study to show the decline – and survival – of parts of the notion of woman represented by Tiraqueau and the Aristotelian voices in Castiglione's dialogue. For this reason, theology and the scholastic notion of woman are examined first, as this may be closely identified with Tiraqueau's outlook. After this, medicine is investigated, followed by ethics and politics, and finally law. It is obvious that so extensive a survey is intended to treat only the most prominent questions, and makes no pretence of completeness. Its justification lies in the belief that authoritative texts were influential throughout the Renaissance, that scholarship was not confined within disciplines, and that throughout Europe there was a form of debate and enquiry which sought interdisciplinary and universal validity for its interpretation of the world.

2

Theology, mystical and occult writings

2.1.1 ｜ It is convenient to examine Renaissance attitudes to woman in theology and mystical writing principally in the light of scholasticism. There are several reasons for doing this: the problems considered and the methods of biblical analysis remain essentially the same for scholastics and Renaissance theologians alike; the influence of the Fathers is strong in both Catholic and reformed writing; furthermore, the scholastics' practice of drawing comparisons with Roman Law, Aristotelian medicine and ethics is continued in the Renaissance. There is no need for the purposes of this study to distinguish between systematic theology (strongly influenced, even in the case of Lutherans, by Aquinas[1]) and biblical commentary, practised widely by theologians of all persuasions. It might be said that post-Tridentine Catholic commentators were more traditional in approach, whereas reformers were more insistent on the 'claritas Scripturae', and more concerned with achieving commonsense explanations of obscurities and plain exegesis for the widest possible public, but this is true only in the most general terms.[2] A small difference between Catholic and reformed writers may be discerned by the latters' exclusion from the canon of apocryphal (deuterocanonical) books, especially Ecclesiasticus, which contains much material about women; but this difference is not sufficient to create a deep division of approach. For both Catholic and reformed theologians, the habit of total recuperation of the text (that is, the desire to make every statement fit into a coherent scheme) remains the same.

2.1.2 The definition of woman (*inter alia*) in books of biblical *loci communes* (a post-Tridentine phenomenon, intended principally for the use of preachers) is relevant to this study insofar as a view of woman emerges from the selection of commonplaces made by the compiler. This selection, which may be favourable or unfavourable to women,[3] is usually based on the appearance of the words *mulier* and *femina* in the vulgate text; there are, however, many important texts in which these words do not appear (e.g. Eph. 4: 13; see below, 2.6.1). Equally, there are texts in which female behaviour is described or evoked obliquely. Finally there are passages of narration and dialogue from which matters pertaining to sex difference may be deduced. While these commonplace books are useful to this study, their principal purpose is moralistic insofar as they treat woman, and they are less concerned with notions than with admonishment.

2.1.3   In scholastic commentary and theology, a variety of inter-pretations of a single passage is made possible by reference to the 'four levels of meaning': literal, tropological, allegorical and anagogical.[4] Renaissance Catholic theologians retain this method of exegesis, and add to it terms taken from the humanistic language arts (e.g. metonomy). Thus, for example, Cornelius a Lapide (1567–1637) records a variety of interpretations of the biblical 'Alphabet of the Good Woman' (Prov. 31: 10–29).[5] 'Woman' is a term with strong figurative associations, as will be seen. She is connected also with the practice of alternate eulogy and vituperation, found in Ecclus. 25 and 26, in certain Fathers of the Church (notably St John Chrysostom[6]) and in moralistic writing of the Middle Ages and Renaissance (see below, 2.7.3). Such excessive praise and invective can be seen in figurative terms (virtue is good, sin is bad: woman becomes a figure for virtue and sin in turn), or can be interpreted as the contradictory nature of woman who is able to plumb the depths of sin and rise to peaks of virtue not accessible to the male.[7] This double possibility is considered by Renaissance theologians whenever the paradoxical nature of female virtue comes into question (see below, 2.11.2).

2.1.4   This chapter will begin with an account of the scholastic notion of woman; next, the scholastics' justifications for considering woman as inferior to man will be recorded, as well as Renaissance discussion of this topic. After this, a series of related questions will be examined which arise from the notion of inferiority. Is woman a human being? Is she made in the image of God? In what form will she be resurrected? How does woman relate to man in matters of sin and malediction? What disqualifications does she suffer in the life of the Church? In what ways is she the equal of man? In what ways is she his superior? This final section will contain some discussion of *theologia platonica* and neoplatonism.

2.2.1   Although the marriage of Aristotle and theology is con-summated in the work of St Thomas Aquinas, there are precedents for this union, notably Alexander of Hales's *Summa*, and indeed, from the earliest Latin Fathers, strongly implied syncretism. It is therefore in no way a shock to the body theological when the physical and ethical aspects of Aristotelianism are married to exegesis or systematic theology. In the distinction of male and female may be discerned Aristotle's general tendency to produce dualities in which one element is superior and the other inferior. The male principle in nature is associated with active, formative and perfected characteristics, while the female is passive, material and deprived, desiring the male in order to become complete. The duality male/female is therefore paralleled by the dualities active/passive, form/matter, act/potency, perfection/imperfection, completion/incompletion, possession/deprivation.[8] In a celebrated passage of the *De generatione animalium* (II.3 [838*a* 27]; cf. IV.6 [775*a* 15f]) Aristotle describes the female as ἐστὶ πεπηρωμένον ; the Latin formulations most frequently encountered are '[Quasi]mas laesus', 'animal occasionatum'.

2.2.2   The Philosopher's argument runs thus: nature would always wish to create the most perfect thing, which is the most completely formed, the best endowed with powers of procreation, and the hottest. Such a creature is the male, who implants his semen in the female to the end of procreating males. If, however, there is some lack of generative heat, or if climatic conditions are adverse, then creation is not perfected and a female results. Aristotle, according to Aquinas, does not mean by this that females are against the intention of nature, because both sexes are necessary to procreation;[9] but that, as regards the individual, females are the result of a generative event not carried through to its final conclusion. The physiological and anatomical implications of this will be discussed elsewhere (3.3.1–3.3.9); for his own purposes, Aquinas synthesizes this understanding of Aristotle (which is that also of Albertus Magnus[10]) with the account of the creation of woman ('productio mulieris') in Genesis (1:26–7, 2:22–3):

It seems that woman ought not to have been produced in the original production of things. For Aristotle says that the female is an incomplete version of the male. But nothing incomplete or defective should have been produced in the first establishment of things; so woman ought not to have been produced then . . . Only as regards nature in the individual is woman something defective and *manqué*. For the active power of the seed of the male tends to produce something like itself, perfect in masculinity; but the procreation of a female is the result either of the debility of the active power, or of some unsuitability of the material, or of some change effected by external influences, like the south wind, for example, which is damp, as we are told in *De generatione animalium*. But with reference to nature in the species as a whole, the female is not something *manqué*, but is according to the plan of nature [*intentio naturae*], and is directed to the work of procreation. Now the tendency of the nature of a species as a whole derives from God, who is the general author of nature. And therefore when he established nature, he brought into being not only the male but the female too.[11]

2.2.3   While this account is most often quoted by subsequent theologians, it is not the only explanation provided: the Dominican Thomas de Vio, Cardinal Cajetan (1469–1534), in his commentary on Gen. 2:21, invokes the metaphorical sense of the verses:

What philosophers have said about the production of woman [that she is a botched male] is recounted metaphorically by Moses. There is a great difference between the point of view of philosophers and that of Moses; for the former considered the production of woman only in relation to sex, whereas Moses considered the production of woman not only as it concerns sex but also with regard to moral behaviour as a whole [*universam vitam moralem*]. Therefore he used a complex metaphor ... as the sleep of Adam should be understood metaphorically, Adam is described asleep, not being woken up or keeping vigil. A deep sleep is sent by God into the man from whom woman is to be produced, and this defect of male power bears a likeness from which woman is naturally produced. For a sleeping man is only half a man; similarly, the principle creating woman is only semi-virile. It is for this reason that woman is called an imperfect version of the male by philosophers.[12]

Another biblical text associated with Gen. 2:21 is 1 Pet. 3:7 (woman the 'weaker vessel') from which scholastics deduce diminished mental powers (especially reason) in the female.[13]

2.2.4   In the Renaissance, three reactions to Aquinas's statement of woman's imperfection may be discerned. The first is direct quotation without further commentary;[14] the second is omission of any discussion of the topic, which may indicate either indifference to scholastic procedures and aims (as is probably the case of Jean Calvin and Conrad Pellikan), or embarrassment (as in the case of Cornelius a Lapide; see below, 2.3.2). The third reaction, hostility, is found in Martin Luther's commentary on Genesis (1:27), in which the Reformer declares that woman is in no way a botched male, but rather those who accuse her of being such 'are themselves monsters and the sons of monsters' for decrying a creature made by God 'with the care he might have devoted to his most noble work'.[15] This hostility to Aristotle and Aquinas contrasts with his avowed belief in the inferiority of woman to man:

Lest woman should seem to be excluded from all glory of future life, Moses mentions both sexes [in Gen. 1:26–7]; it is evident therefore that woman is a different animal to man, not only having different members, but also being far weaker in intellect [*ingenium*]. But although Eve was a most noble creation, like Adam, as regards the image of God, that is, in justice, wisdom and salvation, she was none the less a woman. For as the sun is more splendid than the moon (although the moon is also a most splendid body), so also woman, although the most beautiful handiwork of God, does not equal the dignity and glory of the male.[16]

Luther also refers playfully in his *Tischreden* to the scholastic belief that the different shape of men and women is accountable to the latters' imperfect formation,[17] claiming that it is not because of insufficient generative heat and body temperature that women have wide hips and narrow shoulders, but rather a sign that they have little wisdom and should stay in the home.[18] There is, then, little consistency in his views on this matter. By the seventeenth century, some theologians have taken cognizance of the rejection in medical circles of the concept of sexual imperfection (see below, 3.3.5), and are able to reject in turn the scholastic synthesis of Aristotle and Genesis.[19] This represents a refinement of exegetical techniques, by which scientific and historical elements in Scripture become subject to reassessment. The *terminus ad quem* of this development is often said to be the publication of Richard Simon's *Histoire critique du Vieux Testament* (1678), although stirrings of such an approach are not uncommon in commentaries during the Renaissance.[20] For all this, there is no serious challenge to Aquinas's account of the creation of woman at this time: at best, it might be said that the issue was of no great interest to the majority of Renaissance theologians.

2.3.1   The superiority of man over woman is systematized in various theological tracts in the Middle Ages. In Alexander of Hales's *Summa*, four reasons are given: man is superior to woman because he is active and she is passive (the active is always more honourable than the passive)[21]; because woman is subordinate to man by the curse laid upon her at the Fall (Gen. 3:16); because woman, being constructed physically to feed her offspring, is less robust than man; finally because the 'spiritual signification' (or anagogical meaning) of sex difference lies in the parallel between woman and the soul and man and the Godhead (1 Cor. 11:5–15, 1 Tim. 2:9–15, Eph. 5:22–23).[22] St Bonaventura produces three reasons for man's superiority in his discussion of Peter Lombard's *Sententiae*, III.12 (whether God might have assumed the female sex): man has greater dignity *in principiando* (all human beings, including the female, emanate from Adam); he is more active than the

female; furthermore, he possesses 'auctoritas in praesidendo'.[23] Nicholas
of Lyra, in his gloss on 1 Cor. 11:7, also produces four reasons, three in
common with those quoted above: the fourth is 'convenientia in
natura', by which pre-eminence must be given to one or other of the
members of the same species.[24] These reasons may of course be found,
unsystematically stated, in various Church Fathers. To some degree, this
natural and mystical inferiority of woman answers the question of
whether Eve was the equal or the inferior of Adam before the Fall,
which is mentioned by some Renaissance theologians.[25]

2.3.2   One of the most positive statements against these schematic
accounts of woman's inferiority seems to be that by Cornelius a Lapide
in his commentary on 1 Cor. 11:7 ('the woman is the glory of the man')
which is one of the biblical cornerstones of the scholastics on this topic.
After having briefly stated the meaning of this passage ('woman is made
to the glory of man, and from man, as his creation and image; hence she
is subject to him, and should cover her head as a sign of this subjection'),
he adds a 'note':

Woman, insofar as she is a wife, is the glory of man, that is his glorious image, as I
said above: because God formed woman, that is Eve, from man, and in man's
likeness, so that she might represent man as a copy of him, and be as it were his
image. But woman is not in the full sense of the word the image of man, if we
talk of image in the sense of mind and intellect, by which woman like man is
endowed with a rational soul, intellect, will, memory and freedom, and can
acquire, just as man, all wisdom, grace and glory. For woman is equal to man in
possessing a rational soul, and both, that is woman and man, are made in the
image of God. But she is the image of man in a restrictive and analogical sense;
because woman was made from man, after man, inferior to him and in his
likeness. It is for this reason that St Paul does not say explicitly 'woman is the
image of man', but rather 'woman is the glory of man'; because without doubt,
as Alfonso Salmeron rightly pointed out, woman is an excellent ornament of
man since she is granted to man not only to help him to procreate children, and
administer the family, but also in possession and, as it were, in dominion, over
which man may exercise his jurisdiction and authority. For the authority of
man extends not only to inanimate things and brute beasts, but also to
reasonable creatures, that is, women and wives.[26]

Although this clearly states that in the literal sense woman is the equal of
man, Cornelius a Lapide nonetheless preserves her inferiority in the
metaphorical sense, and even elsewhere in the literal sense (see below,
2.9.1). Like other Renaissance theologians, he does not abandon
altogether the notion of the superiority of man.

2.4.1   The question 'Is woman a human being?' is closely related to, and to some degree answered by, the preceding sections of this chapter. The doctrine of woman the misbegotten male suggests that woman is at once 'not in the ordinary course of Nature [*praeter naturam*]' and not necessarily of the same species as man. In one text, as A. Mitterer has shown, Aquinas associates women with 'other monsters of Nature',[27] but the association relates only to their individual nature and not to the general plan of Nature.[28] One theory of the creation of woman, that Adam was androgynous, and that his female half was separated from him during sleep, is refuted in Augustine and all subsequent ortho-dox commentators,[29] although it must have held a strong appeal for Renaissance neoplatonists (see below, 2.11.4). It would necessarily imply (as Adam, the image of God, was man–woman) that God was also androgynous; this idea, gnostic in origin, reappears in the work of Paracelsus and even in marginal theology.[30] Hermaphrodites are, however, firmly placed in the category of monsters by Renaissance physiologists (see below, 3.5.5). For the scholastics, woman is quite clearly a human being: there is only one theological text (quite possibly spurious) which suggests that she is not.[31]

2.4.2   There is one notable debate on this subject in the Renaissance. In 1595 an anonymous work entitled *Disputatio nova contra mulieres, qua probatur eas homines non esse* ('A new disputation against women, in which it is proved that they are not human beings') was published in Germany. It is possibly the work of the scholar Valens Acidalius (d. 1595), although he strenuously denies this.[32] It achieved considerable notoriety, provoking refutations not only from theologians[33] but also from doctors and jurists.[34] Its appearance nearly coincides with a report of a sermon preached at Lichfield in England on the same theme.[35] John Donne's *Juvenilia*, written at about this time, contain a paradox on the same topic.[36] The text of the *Disputatio nova*, with Simon Gediccus's refutation, is republished at the Hague in 1638, 1641 and 1644, at Paris in 1683, 1690, 1693, at Leipzig in 1707, and without indication of place of printing (and with a different refutation) in 1690. A German version in the form of a dialogue between a (feminist) Jesuit and a (anti-feminist) Benedictine appears in 1615 (reprinted in 1643);[37] an Italian translation is printed in 1647, and a French translation in 1744. The debate is known to Pierre Bayle and Gerard Vossius.[38]

2.4.3   The *Disputatio nova* is a satirical pamphlet directed against the bibliolatry (that is, rigorously literal understanding of the Bible) of anabaptists, and is intended to parallel their statement that Christ was no more than a man with the (lesser) claim that woman is not a human being. While referring incidentally to the scholastic belief in *mas occasionatus* (thesis XLI), the author concentrates on *argumenta e nihilo* and tendentious biblical exegesis to prove his case. The texts which he finds most helpful are Gen. 1:26–7 (no explicit statement that woman is made in the image of God), Gen. 2:21–3 (the creation of woman), Gen. 3:16 (the subordination of Eve to Adam), Eph. 4:13 (the use of *vir* and not *homo* to designate the saved); 1 Tim. 2:15 (the woman's salvation lies in the procreation of males). The *argumenta e nihilo* include the absence of women's names in biblical genealogies, the fact that no woman is described as *homo* in Holy Writ, the fact that there is no mention of the resurrection or damnation of a woman. This last argument is false (see Acts 5:10), and illustrates the satire underlying the theses of this disputation, which the author explicitly declares to be an attack on anabaptism. Like its parallels in satire (see below, 3.2.2) and law (see below, 5.2.1) it provokes nothing but refutation: indeed it is more informative about the function of intellectual jokes in the Renaissance (see below, 6.2.2) than about woman.

2.5.1　　Is woman made in the image of God? The Pauline interpretation of Gen. 1:26–7 (1 Cor. 11:7) seems to allow for a doubt to exist on this question: in the Western Church, first Augustine, then Aquinas clarify this doubt.[39] Woman is made in the image of God insofar as image is understood to mean 'an intelligent nature'; but insofar as man and not woman is, like God, the beginning and end (of woman), woman is not in God's image, but in man's image, being created *ex viro propter virum*. It is therefore by grace, and not by nature, that woman is in God's image, for it is grace which accords an intelligent nature to every human being. As R. Metz points out, the distinction man/woman parallels the distinctions grace/nature and invisible/visible Church.[40] Renaissance writers nearly all refer to Augustine's definition of image in *De trinitate*,[41] which allows woman, according to Marin Mersenne's interpretation, three faculties of mind: passive intellect (=memory), active intellect and will.[42] Like the statement by Cornelius a Lapide on the equality of the sexes (see above, 2.3.2), this attribution of qualities seems to be inconsistent with Aristotelian ethics (see below, 4.3.1–4.3.8). Johann Gerhard and other Lutherans argue that the sense of 1 Cor. 11:7 can best be seen in the light of Gen. 3:16 and 1 Pet. 3:7, and that the text indicates no more than woman's dependence on man;[43] Peter Martyr Vermigli finds an allegorical interpretation of the same text which relates to both sexes (we are males when we study God, females when

we immerse ourselves in human affairs), but he also repeats a version of
Augustine's definition of image (knowledge of God and justice).[44]
There are certain moral theologians who profess to doubt whether
woman is made in the image of God, but only as a ploy by which to
castigate female vanity and the evils of cosmetics and finery.[45] Thus, in
the Renaissance, a restrictive understanding of image which allows the
male pre-eminence over the female is retained from patristic and
scholastic discussions.

2.6.1   In what form are women to be resurrected? The biblical *loci*
which give rise to this question are Matt. 22:29–30 (marriage in
heaven); 1 Cor. 15:24 (no subjection in heaven; therefore women must
be changed into men in order to be equal to men); Eph. 4:13 (the saved
are resurrected as 'perfect males'); Gal. 3:28 (sex in heaven). This
eschatalogical question relates to the condition of the saved, which is
perfect, free from subjection and sin. Now woman is an imperfect
creation subject to her husband. In the early Church, there are debates on
this topic, and a disagreement between Greek and Latin Fathers;[46] after
Augustine's comments in *The City of God*, there seems to be a lull in the
discussions.[47] Peter Lombard in his *Sententiae* (IV.44) argues that woman
is to be resurrected as a woman and made perfect as such; this opinion is
adopted by Bonaventura[48] and by Aquinas, who points out that once
the biblical curse (Gen. 3:16) is lifted and 'natural' inferiority removed,
there would be no difference in the status of the sexes in heaven.[49] One
text (Eph. 4:13 'till we all come ... unto a perfect man') causes
particular difficulty, which is resolved either by reference to the sense of
vir (that is *virtus*), or to the sense of the whole verse, which, according to
Calvin, indicates that the saved will be in all respects Christ-like.[50]
Renaissance commentators record this debate, and seem unanimously to
agree that woman will be resurrected as a woman.[51]

2.6.2   An interesting apparent dissension from this unanimity is that of
Duns Scotus, who, according to some commentators, says in his
commentary on Peter Lombard's *Sententiae* that all women will become
men in heaven, except for the Virgin Mary.[52] In the mid fifteenth
century, Alphonsus Tostatus, Bishop of Avila, refutes this view at length
in his commentary on Genesis.[53] Renaissance editors of Scotus deny
strenuously that he wrote this, and claim that it is an interpolation which
other Renaissance theologians have failed to identify.[54] The exception of
the Virgin Mary has, of course, its own special significance (see below,
2.11.3). Some late Renaissance commentators scorn the whole question
as futile;[55] others (notably Gerhard and Cornelius a Lapide) follow the

scholastic arguments, but add a eulogy of the female sex to them,[56] indicating again a desire to improve the status of woman in theology without tampering with the conceptual structure or with the notion of her inferiority to man.

2.7.1   The relationship between sin and sex difference produces less unified debates. The prototype of discussions on this topic is provided by the question of whether Adam or Eve was more responsible for the Fall. Peter Lombard rehearses arguments for and against the proposition that Eve sinned more than Adam, and he is followed in this by subsequent commentators on the *Sententiae* and by Aquinas. There is no clear answer to the question; Eve has weaker powers of reason than Adam, so less may be expected of her; but on the other hand, she alone is deceived, and it is she who becomes, in Tertullian's phrase, the door of the devil (*janua diaboli*).[57] It is for this reason (the association of temptation and seduction with women's speech) that the female sex is prohibited from speaking in church (see below, 2.8.1). A parallel debate, in which the same arguments are produced, is that which concerns the relative responsibility of the sexes in adultery. Peter Martyr Vermigli writes on this in the Renaissance, and his conclusions reflect both respect for scholastic thought and a slight lessening of the burden of sin for women. He declares himself satisfied with the scholastic distinction of adultery according to its relation to conjugal fidelity (in which both sexes sin equally), or to the responsibility to be expected from the individual (in which man sins the greater), or to the harmful effects on family life (in which woman is more culpable than man). At the same time, he acknowledges that it is the duty of the man to set an example and to control his wife, and that if she is blamed more by society for her lapse, it is because the sin is often visible in her, for she may become pregnant.[58]

2.7.2   On the question of specific female vices, a more amorphous debate is encountered. The desire for ornaments, cosmetics and other enhancements of beauty, much discussed in the early Church, is thought to be a failing peculiar to women by Jerome, who argues at one point that it might be considered as theologically indifferent provided that it is divorced from vanity and lechery.[59] Aquinas rehearses the same argument,[60] and it appears in an even more liberal form in the work of the enlightened moralist St Francis of Sales (1567–1622).[61] The biblical *loci* are 1 Cor. 7:34 (St Paul's statement that, unlike the unmarried, wives care for the things of this world, and try to please their husbands) and 1 Tim. 2:9 (a recommendation of modesty and sobriety in dress). As well as in systematic theology and biblical commentary, there is a copious literature of admonishments to women about self-adornment. It points out the political dangers of luxury (see below, 4.6.1, for the association of women and political degeneration through over-spending), the inherent sins of vanity, pride and lechery (which are committed if, as is assumed to be the case, women are dressing to please not their husbands but other men), and the falsification of values involved in corsetry and cosmetics (often associated with arguments of a neoplatonist character about the identity of virtue and natural beauty: see below, 2.11.4).[62] Among Renaissance commentators, Calvin points out that men no less than women are enjoined to forswear vain and licentious clothing and ornaments.[63] A further specifically female vice is garrulity, associated, as has been seen, with the Fall, but castigated independently in ancient Greek writing: this will be examined further in another context (see below, 4.4.3).

2.7.3   One may also find description of female vice in general in patristic and scholastic writing, repeated by Renaissance moralists. St Antoninus Forciglioni's alphabet of female vices (a counter-alphabet to the biblical Hebrew alphabet of female virtues (Prov. 31:10–29)) encompasses almost the whole domain of sin, and suggests that not only are the vices listed found in woman, but also that they hold greater sway over her than over man.[64] This alphabet is well known in the Renaissance, and appears in Spanish, French, English and Dutch versions, usually without reference to its scholastic source.[65] The excessive denunciation of woman (sometimes coupled with fulsome eulogy) is found in certain Church Fathers, notably Tertullian and Chrysostom, both of whom produce passages in which the question 'quid est mulier?' is answered by a long series of epithets.[66] When this condemnation of the *mala mulier* (sometimes *meretrix*) is combined with praise of the *bona mulier*, there seems to be a suggestion that in the case of woman there is no moderation or middle ground of vice and virtue (see above, 2.1.3). This may be connected with the paradoxical nature of female virtue (see below, 2.11.2); but in any case, it is clear that the Renaissance did not cease the practice of denouncing 'female vice', even if they considered it to be equally shared by men.

2.7.4   In the metaphorical and allegorical understanding of biblical texts, woman is often identified with sensuality.[67] Once Adam's eyes have been opened (Gen. 3:7), woman in her person becomes an incitation to lust and concupiscence, and it is not uncommon in theological tracts to find the advice that men should shun women's company at all times for this reason.[68] Bonaventura, it is true, provides a justification for the contemplation of women, in claiming that through their beauty it is possible to communicate with God[69] (an argument reminiscent of neoplatonism: see below, 2.11.4); but such arguments are rare in scholastic writings. As well as being the passive object of lust, woman can also instigate it; the *mulier blandiens* (sometimes *meretrix*) is subjected to violent diatribes in the Old Testament (Ecclus. 25:17–36; Prov. 6:24–6) and in books of commonplaces for the use of post-Tridentine preachers (see above, 2.1.2). One such biblical text much debated by Catholic writers is Ecclus. 42:14: 'Better is the wickedness of a man than a pleasant-dealing woman [*mulier bene faciens*]'. Various interpretations are offered for this: in scholastic writing, 'woman' is here understood metaphorically to indicate human frailty (*infirmitas*) in general, and early Renaissance commentators adopt the same understanding. A seventeenth-century French preacher manages to produce an interpretation which, paradoxically, enhances the honour of woman:

It seems that when the author of Ecclesiasticus produced this enigma, or rather, this paradox, he wanted by using a marvellous, almost divine strategy to counterbalance the pride and presumption of women who by their nature were swollen with vanity and self-love; by a holy act of deceit, and employing a remedy more salutary than it was pleasant, he pretended to hold even their virtue in contempt, clearly foreseeing that they would find means and ways of rising even higher than they had to, and of adding greatly to it.[70]

In most texts, however, the association of woman with sin through her beauty is not denied. The most potent refutation of this is to be found in neoplatonist writing, where the beauty of the female body is said to reflect the beauty of the soul, making beauty no longer an *occasio peccati* but rather a step on the ladder to divine love (see below, 2.11.4). As far as I know, no direct link is drawn by a Renaissance theologian between Ecclus. 42:14 and neoplatonist arguments about beauty. The absence of such a link may well indicate embarrassment about the uneasy relationship between some pagan texts and the Bible, which can be sensed elsewhere (see below, 3.4.1).

2.7.5   The curse laid upon woman at the Fall (Gen. 3:16) inflicts on her three ills: pain in matters relating to procreation, sadness, and subjection to her husband.[71] According to one Renaissance theologian, the injunction that Adam must work applies to Eve also.[72] One aspect of the curse on woman concerns the physiological differences of the sexes. Woman, in Judaic law, is polluted by menstruation and childbirth (Lev.

12:2–5; Lev. 15:19–27), and the association of woman and uncleanness is carried over into Christianity. Though the disqualification from communion and the touching of sacred vessels at such times of uncleanness, and the exclusion from certain sacred places, relate only to the physiology of woman, she is nonetheless put at a disadvantage to man thereby, whether in herself saintly or sinful. The taboo relating to woman's 'natural infirmity' is linked consciously with original sin by scholastics, as well as with the peripatetic notion of imperfection.[73] Renaissance writers on this subject do not seem to abandon such beliefs, with the exception of some English puritans.[74] Of sixteenth-century continental theologians, Luther alone seems to make positive statements about woman's malediction, calling it a 'joyful punishment' because of the joys of maternity which remain after its unpleasantness, and the hope of eternal life associated with procreation (1 Tim. 2:15).[75]

2.8.1   In the life of the Church, various other disqualifications emanate from the curse and Eve's behaviour. Scholastics point out that women must cover their heads in church as a sign of submission (1 Cor. 11:5–7),[76] and their arguments are repeated by Renaissance writers, one of whom (Calvin) points to other reasons for this act: bald women are monstrous, and those with fine heads of hair might incite men to lustful thoughts in church.[77] Woman is debarred from speaking (because Eve's words beguiled Adam),[78] from teaching and from preaching (1 Tim. 2:11–12). She is excluded from the priesthood and its functions of hearing confessions and administering sacraments.[79] Renaissance canon lawyers indicate the cases in which abbesses may exercise these powers by proxy, but there is no defence of woman priests (the medieval woman bishop (possibly apocryphal) of Apulia is described by Baronius as the 'monstrum Apuliae'[80]). The idea is mooted in some English theological writing, as is the idea of the woman preacher, but both can only be condoned, it seems, because of their exceptional nature.[81] Woman remains excluded from the administration of the spiritual life of the Church except in cases of special grace (see below, 2.10.1).

2.9.1   The most burdensome and wide-ranging effect of the malediction of Eve is the subjection of women to their husbands. In scholastic writing, woman is generally considered to have been naturally inferior to man before the Fall.[82] Even Luther, who does not accept the peripatetic argument of female imperfection, argues that Eve is inferior to Adam as is the moon to the sun (see above, 2.2.4). There are some English puritans who argue that before the Fall the sexes were equal, and even some feminist writers who insist (possibly facetiously) that if subjection is a punishment, it must represent the removal of authority; therefore woman was superior to man in the Garden of Eden.[83] In more serious writings, however, the full array of biblical texts relating to subordination are reviewed: Gen. 3 : 16, 1 Cor. 11 : 5–15, 1 Tim. 2 : 9–15, Eph. 5 : 22–23, 1 Pet. 3 : 7. These texts are in almost complete harmony with pagan tracts on the same topic, of which the pseudo-Aristotelian *Economics* and Plutarch's *Conjugalia praecepta* are the most quoted by Renaissance theologians.[84] Neither of these texts was known in its entirety to scholastic writers, although Church Fathers rehearse the same arguments, and other relevant passages, notably from Aristotle's *Politics*, were available to them. In the *Politics* (1.1 ; see below, 4.5.4) wives are distinguished from slaves, and even if one Augustinian text seems to suggest that there is no difference in status,[85] both medieval and Renaissance commentators insist on the distinction. It is also inferred from the subordination of Eve that woman should not play any part in the running of the state or in public affairs, but should occupy herself with 'woman's work'. Nicholas of Lyra relates the usurpation of inappropriate sexual rôles to transvestism, and interprets its prohibition in Judaic law (Deut. 22 : 5) as a figure for the exclusion of men and women from each other's social and political functions.[86]

2.9.2   On the question of the status of man in marriage, a shift in emphasis from scholastic to Renaissance writing may be discerned. Woman is created to be not his servant or his mistress but his companion; for this reason she is created from his rib, not his foot or his head. The functions of marriage which relate equally to both partners are mutual help, companionship and procreation.[87] Because of this mutual aim and aid, man is, as it were, the steward (*curator*) of woman in this life, and it is incumbent upon him to love and respect her as much as she is enjoined to love and respect him (Col. 3 : 18–19).[88] This common commitment to the institution and aims of matrimony leads to a reassessment of the married state in Renaissance writing which sets aside the scholastics' grudging justification of marriage as a cure for concupiscence (1 Cor. 7 : 9 'it is better to marry than to burn'), and lays greater emphasis on its comfort and companionship. Such a change of perspective is not unconnected with the doubts expressed about the usefulness of religious celibacy, which in English puritan writing is considered to be an unnatural state (Gen. 2 : 18, 'It is not good that the man should be alone').[89] Prominent Renaissance texts which treat of this rehabilitation of marriage are Erasmus's *Sancti matrimonii institutio* (1526), Henricus

Cornelius Agrippa von Nettesheim's *De sacramento matrimonii declamatio* (1526) and Juan Luis Vives's *De institutione foeminae Christianae* (1523).[90] The rôles of man and woman in matrimony, then, are harmoniously treated by pagan and Christian writers, and by both Catholic and reformed theologians in the Renaissance. There seems to be no room for a revision or a reversal of these rôles (even English puritans, invoking the scholastic argument of *convenientia*, make no attempt to reform marriage to this extent),[91] or of the rôles of man and woman in society; while exceptions both in marriage and society may be tolerated, the rule remains firm and inviolate (see below, 4.5.1–4.5.7).[92]

2.10.1   There are, of course, many areas in which the sexes are equal, relating to actions considered to be theologically indifferent (that is, attracting neither condemnation nor eulogy). These are not mentioned by commentators, and need not concern us here. In theological terms, woman is the equal of man in few respects. As St Clement of Alexandria points out in his *Paedagogus*, the word (*logos*) is as much for women as it is for men;[93] thus the text of the Bible, either heard or read, is as appropriate to them as to men. That they should be urged to read the text is a Renaissance phenomenon; Erasmus, in the liminary prayer (paraclesis) to his edition of the New Testament in Greek (1516) argues eloquently for this, as does Vives in his *De institutione foeminae Christianae*.[94] Reformers take up this recommendation of the evangelical humanists, and seem more enthusiastic about it than their Catholic counterparts.[95] Woman's equality to man emerges also in that the same punishment and reward await both sexes in the next life: this argument, first used by St Basil the Great, is found not infrequently in Renaissance writings on women.[96] The equal part played by woman in redemption is also pointed out: in Peter Lombard's *Sententiae* (III.12) it is asked why God did not assume the female sex in the incarnation, and the answer points to the redemptive rôle of the Virgin Mary, who, as the second Eve, is the instrument of salvation. Much is made of this in Marian literature of the Counter-Reformation, but as will be seen (below, 2.11.3) it is not altogether clear whether the argument works in favour of women as a whole.

2.11.1   There are some domains in which woman's superiority to man is conceded. There are certain virtues which are associated more with women than men: longsuffering, humility, patience, compassion and public charity are of this order.[97] The female sex is also thought to possess devoutness in greater measure than the male: an early Marian prayer includes the phrase 'pray for the devout female sex'.[98] Nicholas of Lyra links this prayer with a verse from the Song of Solomon (5:8);[99] Aquinas also makes reference to it, but claims that the power of devoutness does not lie in a particular mental attribute, but rather in its lack (*defectus contemplationis*); the advantage which accrues to women is that of credulity rather than rational belief.[100] In some ways the gift of prophecy in women may be compared to that of devotion, although it also relates to the paradoxical status of virtue in women (see below, 2.11.2). Women are enjoined not to teach, but they are known to have been prophets; Deborah is one biblical example often cited, as are Elizabeth the mother of John the Baptist and Ann the daughter of Phanuel.[101] When scholastics such as Nicholas of Lyra refer to such women, they are described as 'illuminatae mentis', made lucid, presumably, by special grace.[102] A similar point is made by Renaissance theologians, who point out that women may prophesy privately without infringing divine law, but even then they must be considered as exceptions. Peter Martyr Vermigli is quite clear on this:

I think that it is not to be denied that some women imbued with the gift of prophecy have taught the people in public, passing on to them those things which were revealed to them by God. For divine gifts are not conferred in order to be hidden away, but so that they may promote the edification of the Church as a whole. But it should not be deduced from this that that which God does in some particular case of privilege should be made by us a model of behaviour.[103]

The gift of prophecy calls to mind the Sibyls, whose powers, like those of their biblical counterparts, are celebrated in Renaissance mystical writings.[104]

2.11.2 Prophecy contravenes the prohibition of speech, teaching and preaching by women: it reflects one aspect of a further prerogative of woman over man, which is only conducive to her honour in a rather doubtful way. If woman is generally considered to be weaker than man, her virtuous acts become as a consequence much more admirable, since the gap between her action and her true nature is greater than the same gap in a man. It is clear from a variety of texts that God delights in confounding the mighty by the agency of the weak;[105] Judith, Deborah and Jael among biblical women are all figures for this. The evocation of the disproportion of act and agent is found notably in Peter Abelard's hymns in the medieval period.[106] Other scholastic writers also dwell on this paradox of strength in weakness, although it is sometimes attenuated by reference to the disproportion which exists between the power of grace and human frailty in general.[107] Renaissance theologians, especially after the Council of Trent, delight in this paradox, and associate it both with the duality strength/weakness and with specific female failings and vices which are not only absent in saintly women but even replaced by the corresponding virtues.[108] The trio of vices – ambition, avarice and lechery – which are associated with this world in a verse of the first epistle general of John (2:16),[109] are all linked with woman, who as the worldly creature *par excellence* is thought to be more deeply imbued with them than is man. The counter-virtues of humility, chastity and charity are stressed in the depiction of female saints of the late Renaissance period, as well as in the figure of the Virgin Mary (see below, 2.11.3).[110] It cannot be said, however, that such praise is to the advantage of the mass of women, who, by contrast with these saintly exceptions, remain associated with weaker reason, stronger passions and greater inherent vice.

One of the few tracts to produce a formula wholly to the honour of the female sex is Guillaume Postel's *Les très-merveilleuses victoires des femmes du nouveau monde* (1553). Postel (1505?–1581) argues that woman's weaknesses and imperfections are advantageous to her, since she naturally strives after perfection (whereas man, when he courts woman, courts an object less perfect than himself). By so doing, Postel reverses the normal understanding of strength and weakness. If a weakness is a source of strength, and strength a source of weakness, woman is paradoxically superior to man because she is inferior to him. Furthermore, Postel elaborates a new sexual psychology of some complexity involving such terms as *esprit, mente, anime, âme* which leads to the assertion that woman is the most perfect being because her psychosomatic state is more in harmony with the sublunary world than is the male's.[111] Such a radical theory finds parallels in certain occult neoplatonist and gnostic ideas. Before Postel, Paracelsus (1494–1541) had postulated a Godhead in whom was also a woman, not possessing power, nor a place in the Trinity, but connected with mystical female forces in stones and plants.[112] These forces are systematized in alchemistic writings, and consist in the *corpus* (as opposed to the masculine *spiritus*, and the sexless *anima*) which of itself is imperfect, weak and dead, but is cleansed by the *spiritus* and given life by the *anima*.[113] In such schemata, the influence of Aristotle as well as gnosticism can be quite strongly felt. Postel's theory seems to find no imitator or disciple in the Renaissance. It demonstrates effectively how difficult it was at this time to abandon the scholastic synthesis and methods in favour of some new system without appearing to abandon all connection with contemporary linguistic and philosophical usage.

2.11.3   An even more questionable advantage to womankind is to be found in the figure of the Virgin Mary. Her prominence both in the Middle Ages and the Counter-Reformation is well known; it is only necessary here to give a brief account of her influence on the status of woman. The Virgin Mary is the second Eve, prefigured by all the major female figures of the Old Testament and by the description of the good wife (Prov. 31 : 10–29).[114] Her virtues are those of humility, obedience, silence (Luke 2 : 19; cf. the female vice of garrulity), mortification, modesty, prudence. These are (with the possible exception of the last, see below 4.3.4) in no way inconsistent with traditional female virtue, and Mary can therefore easily be transformed into a perfect model of womanhood. However, as St Peter Canisius points out in his seminal Marian work *De Maria Virgine incomparabili* (1577), she is not like other women in very important ways:

A virgin not sterile, but fertile; married to a man, but made fruitful by God; bearing a son, but knowing not a man; forever inviolate, yet not deprived of progeny. A virgin pregnant but incorrupt, and intact even in childbirth. A virgin before marriage and in marriage, a pregnant virgin, a virgin giving suck, a perpetual virgin. A virgin without concupiscence conceiving the saviour. A virgin bearing a child in the womb without hardship, giving birth to God without pain.[115]

She is, in fact, exempt from all female vice and imperfection, and thus can accede directly to heaven by assumption unlike any other human being. Far from being the glory of her sex, she is not of her sex in its malediction, tribulation and imperfection. She incarnates certain moral virtues which are consistent with the social and religious rôle of women (see below, 4.5.1–4.5.7), but does not ever become a model of behaviour, so remote is she from others of her sex. Her importance to the Counter-Reformation is very great; in many texts and paintings she is linked with feminist topics; but in the final analysis, her relationship to woman is similar to that of Christ to mankind, a model of unattainable perfection. Her virginity, much stressed by Catholic writers, may be linked with the literature which deals with its mystical rights and powers.[116] These apply as much to men as to women, although they are more remarkable in the case of the latter. Physical incorruption plays little or no part, however, in the thought of reformed theologians, who see marriage as a natural state and a religious duty (Gen. 1 : 22).[117] The powers associated with virginity are also linked with pagan mysteries and mythology, notably in the figure of Diana; this is strongly reflected in the visual arts of the Renaissance, as Sir E. H. Gombrich and Edgar Wind have pointed out.[118]

2.11.4   The last advantage of woman over man to be considered here is solely a feature of the Renaissance, although it is consistent with the advantages considered already. Marsilio Ficino's attempt to marry Plato and theology leads him to a reconsideration of divine love which conduces greatly to the honour of the female sex, and it is a commonplace that, in the Renaissance, woman was exalted by neoplatonist theories. Love is the *vinculum mundi*, binding the whole of creation together; earthly love is a step on the ladder of love leading eventually to ecstatic reunion with the Godhead. When a woman is loved, her lover is loving not only her, but God and himself as well. The perfection of love is in reciprocity; but its origin lies in beauty, which women possess in greater store than men. Physical beauty reflects mental goodness; thus women are better than men. Furthermore, the being least weighed down with earthly matter is the most spiritual, and its soul is more free to escape from the fetters of physical existence; women therefore are able more easily to transcend the limitations of this world.[119] In this system of thought – a mystical understanding of life, far removed from Aristotelian physics and the literal understanding of the Bible – woman is released from the disadvantages of her greater weakness, and endowed with spiritual gifts above those of man. She communicates with the angels, as St Clement of Alexandria had pointed out, and she instructs man in the cult of love.[120] This mystical and pedagogical rôle, often associated with virginity, is evoked in Renaissance literature and emblems, notably the pastoral tradition and in works of marginal theology such as Pietro Calanna's *Philosophia seniorum sacerdotia et platonica* (1599), and André Du Chesne's *Figures mystiques du riche et précieux cabinet des dames* (1605).[121] The mutual desire of lovers to mirror themselves in the other's soul ('to die to oneself in order to live again in another') is often associated with the myth of the androgyne (specifically rejected, as has been seen, by scholastic theology) and with the rebirth of the new man in Christ (Rom. 6: 4–6).

It would be difficult to underestimate the intellectual and spiritual fervour to which neoplatonism gave rise, and which penetrated not only theology but also pedagogy and methodology in the guise of Ramism. The effects of this fervour on the intellectual life of Europe are more difficult to assess. It seems that, in the particular case of the status of women, the mystical prerogatives find no translation into lasting advantages or advances. Ficino himself, it should be remembered, writes differently of the female sex in other contexts; he refers to their imperfect physical nature, quoting Aquinas,[122] and declares elsewhere that a wife should be subservient to her husband.[123] His general advice to men and women is even less conducive to the belief that women should be considered superior: 'Let men beware of being in any way effeminate (*muliebris*). Let woman try in some way to be virile and above all else chaste. Just as courage befits a man, so does chastity a woman.'[124] While it is true to say that his system of love is highly influential and revolutionary, it does not seem to bring about a profound change of attitudes towards the relative position of the sexes in the imperfect, sublunary world, although some modification in the mystical notion of woman may be attributable to neoplatonism.

2.12.1   In spite of the influence of neoplatonism, then, the scholastic infrastructure of the Renaissance notion of woman remains intact. This is due in no small part to the strong synthetic nature of the scholastic notion; no other system is evolved which is able to offer as comprehensive an explanation for the biblical commonplaces about woman. It is striking that there is no deep rift of opinion about woman between those writing in the early Renaissance and those writing at its end, nor between Catholic and reformed theologians, although issues of difference (such as general access to the Bible) affect some aspects of this topic and have been adduced as important factors in social change. At first sight, some English puritans seem to cut through the construction of scholastic thought and to suggest new approaches; the following passage from John Wing's *The crowne coniugall* (1620) appears audacious and original when compared with continental thought:

The booke of God maketh mention of *Women* of divers kindes, but all of them ... may be reduced to one of these heads; either the *Mysticall*, *Naturall*, or *Matrimoniall*, Woman. The *Mystical* Woman, is found in the Scriptures to be the embleme or representation of *good* and *evill* ... The next is the NATURALL Woman, by whome we understand the man foeminine, or the female of man- kinde ... The last is the Woman Matrimoniall, and her alone we call a *wife*, being a Woman under marriage, either only *initiate*, in tearms of *contract* or betrothing ... or *compleate*, and *consummate* called *ever* a wife.[125]

There is in this no more than the conjunction of two paradigms normally considered separately: the language paradigm (literal/ tropological/allegorical/anagogical) and the marital paradigm (maiden/ wife/widow) which forms the basis of moralistic writing about women (see below, 4.5.1). Elsewhere in puritan writing, one finds, as much as audacious suggestions about preaching and priests, defence of the subordination of woman in marriage,[126] and, although it has been argued that women improved their position in family and state in England at this time,[127] it seems that there is not a complete liberation from the inherited medieval notions about the female sex.

2.12.2   Various methods of reassessment of evidence, adumbrated at this time, might have offered the means of a radical change in attitudes. The first is the abandonment of the tenet of total recuperation, whereby all biblical texts must be made to fit into a proposed scheme. In insisting on Jerome's doubts about the apocryphal (or deuterocanonical) books, reformed theologians open the way for the pursuit of interpolation elsewhere and a strategy of selection, but this is not pursued.[128] In both Catholic and reformed writing, hints about the historical nature of biblical texts (especially the Pauline epistles) may have suggested to some theologians that statements about women could be considered as relative to the society and *mores* of time and not as absolute religious prescriptions; but again there is no rigorous application of this exegetical method. Textual criticism based on improved language skills and the study of manuscripts, although influential in causing changes in other domains, seem in this sphere to offer few possibilities in the way of reassessment. Finally, the separation of sexual characteristics from gender, which is in fact practised by scholastic theologians ('a manly soul in a weak female body'), seems to result in a pursuit of paradox and a provocation of wonderment in the reader or listener, and not in the development of a new paradigm of psychological characteristics. The paradox strengthens the presumption of female weakness, and acts as a conservative force on language and ideas. Only in works which pass for being heretical or wild in their time, such as Guillaume Postel's *Très-merveilleuses victoires*, can one detect the expression of a system which frees Renaissance thought from its habitual magnetic poles. The use of neologisms ('mente', 'anime') and the redefinition of words with well-established psychological meanings ('esprit', 'âme') seem to permit a fresh assessment of woman, and give some indication of the undercurrent of neoplatonist and gnostic ideas.

2.12.3   The paradigm of marriage – maiden/wife/widow – plays a very important part in the formulation of theological ideas about woman. It is closely connected with the malediction of Eve, as the wife's subordination emanates from her sin; it is also in itself a divine institution with which man may not tamper. As such, it remains an immovable object in the way of change, while religion maintains its authority. Equally important is the paradigm of woman's physiological nature, which in some states confers privileges and dignity (such as motherhood), but in others causes exclusion and prohibition. The third paradigm is provided on a linguistic level by the four levels of meaning in Holy Writ, which allows for total recuperation of statements about the female sex, and which accords to it strong figurative and mystical associations. The first two of these three paradigms often act in conjunction; they imply contraries (married/unmarried, clean/unclean) which belong to Zabarella's 'species contraria immediata' (see above, 1.1.4). Just as a woman cannot be simultaneously clean and unclean, married and unmarried, so also does the difference of sex in theological terms exclude intermediates; sex is a polarity rather than something which admits ranges of possibilities to both man and woman which may overlap. Only in psychological terms can apparent contradiction or paradox arise ('a manly soul/a womanly body'), and here it can be resolved by recourse to the argument of special grace (see above, 2.11.1), or the exception which emerges from the necessity of nature but not its intention (see Chap. 2 n. 9). One may note therefore in theological studies of the Renaissance period an adherence to firm divisions and an aversion to ambiguity or complex relationships. This has been seen to apply to both neoscholastic and reformed commentaries; although these are at variance on many fundamental theological issues, it seems that they share this feature of the intellectual infrastructure of their age.

2.12.4   It emerges from this study that the scholastic notion of woman is modified only slightly by Renaissance theologians and commentators. It seems generally accepted that woman is not quite the equal of man in the manner of her creation. Even when the *mas occasionatus* theory is abandoned, this belief is generally adhered to, for different reasons (see above, 2.3.1, 2.7.1). Most writers suggest that woman is less well endowed with moral apparatus, and continue the practice of praising saintly women for their paradoxical virtue. But, like woman's subordination to her husband and her disqualification from full participation in the spiritual life, this inequality is attached to this life only, and all commentators stress that she will share equally in the joys of paradise. In theological terms woman is, therefore, the inferior of the male by nature, his equal by grace.

3

Medicine, anatomy, physiology

3.1.1   The subject of woman as seen by physiologists, anatomists and physicians is complex and multifaceted, because of its contiguity (and coincidence) with spermatology, hysterology, the science of the humours and theories of physical change. It is also very closely related to embryology, which exercises a deep influence on medical discussions about woman, and even determines to some degree the series of problems considered by medieval and Renaissance writers. In the excellent accounts of ancient embryology by Erna Lesky[1] and H. B. Adelmann,[2] this fact is pointed out, and the principal questions are listed: what is the origin of semen? do both sexes produce it? which part of the body develops first in the foetus? what determines sex and resemblance of children to parents? These questions give rise to a set of *loci classici* which are discussed by Renaissance doctors.

3.1.2   Renaissance medicine is distinct from the medieval discipline not only because of the work of humanists who produce the great editions, indices and commentaries of Aristotle, Hippocrates and Galen in the first half of the sixteenth century, but also because of the growth of experimental anatomy. The work of Andreas Vesalius, Gabriele Falloppio and Realdo Colombo is paralleled in the clinical sphere by the producers of *consilia* (case histories) and great writers on physiology, among them Jean Fernel. Although most doctors refer to ancient sects (the 'practici' who follow Averroes, the 'peripatetici', the 'Galenici', the 'methodici', the 'empirici'), the vast majority of them are, according to Adelmann, 'thoroughgoing Galenists at heart',[3] but influenced to different degrees by Aristotle, Avicenna and Hippocrates. It is this last for whom the greatest respect is shown. Where his texts are thought to be erroneous, interpolation is invoked (see below, 3.3.7); Aristotle is sometimes described as his vulgar plagiarist.[4] Peripatetic doctors, working on the new published texts of the Philosopher, set out to defend him, but differ in their interpretations, as will be seen (below, 3.4.2). The 'neoterici' (doctors of the modern school), working from observation and experiment, attack all ancient authorities, but are not altogether free from inherited beliefs and structures of thought.[5] The situation by the end of the sixteenth century is quite confused, but it may be said with a certain degree of confidence that the general context of medicine remains Galenist, while the work of Aristotle and the 'neoterici' is in dispute, leading to accusations of incompetence and plagiarism. Such accusations are found in the *De universa mulierum medicina* of Rodrigues de Castro (1546?–1627), published in 1603; he denounces the sixteenth-century collection of medical texts on woman entitled *Gynaecea* as 'an amalgam of excellent doctrine and wild speculation which could easily mislead students of medicine',[6] yet he himself relies heavily on some parts of it. The *Gynaecea*, which first appears in 1566, and is expanded in later editions (1577, 1586–7, 1597) is an extremely useful document for the purposes of this study. It assembles the major writings on woman not only of antiquity and the Middle Ages, but also of contemporaries.[7] It shows that the most prolific period of writing comes after the great editions of medical authorities and the publication of the findings of anatomists (*c.* 1540–1600), and that such writing is undertaken in France, Spain, Germany and Italy.

3.1.3   This rather confused situation produces, in the case of medical disputes about woman, the curious combination of doctors claiming to be Galenists and feminists: that is, believing 'against Aristotle' that men and women are equally perfect in their sex (see below, 3.3.5). The combination is curious, because Galen himself does not claim this; it becomes even more bizarre, when theology in the form of the Aristotelian Aquinas is invoked as further evidence of the equality of the sexes.[8] Many doctors at the end of the sixteenth and the beginning of the seventeenth centuries write eloquently against the wrong done to the honour of woman by Aristotle,[9] and it is possible to argue that there is a feminist movement in medical spheres, where in theology there is little evidence of one. The contradictions involved in this movement will emerge in the course of the chapter. But reliance on ancient authorities and deep structures of thought, such as the Pythagorean opposites which are strongly in evidence in ancient texts on woman (see above, 1.1.3), produce a matrix as inescapable as the scholastic synthesis. The problem unique to Renaissance doctors, 'to harmonize the received texts with a growing body of fresh knowledge that renewed and increasingly more intensive and extensive observations were every day bringing to their notice',[10] leads even conservative doctors such as Jean Riolan the Elder to state that 'it is absurd to combat observation and experience with reason out of respect for antiquity'.[11] But observation can only affect the tenets of medical science if such instruments as the microscope make it possible; in embryology and gynaecology, the major developments are all post-1650 (Reinier de Graaf, Karl Ernst von Baer[12]). Until these breakthroughs, the questions asked of the evidence available were not necessarily the most profitable ones, as they emerge not so much from observation as from a conceptual framework inherited from the ancients.

3.1.4   It may be helpful at this point briefly to recapitulate Aristotle's and Galen's ideas on woman. According to the former's theory, a male animal is one that generates in another, whereas the female generates in herself.[13] She is further characterized by deprived, passive and material traits, cold and moist dominant humours and a desire for completion by intercourse with the male.[14] This is essentially the medieval understanding of Aristotle, as P. Diepgen has shown;[15] it has been seen how such notions are syncretized with Christian thought. Galen differs in one essential point (the existence and efficacy of female semen: see below 3.4.1–3.4.3); this idea was known in the medieval period, but not developed.[16] His account of woman in the *De usu partium corporis* (XIV) is otherwise in harmony with peripatetic teaching, which is enriched by him with a more extensive theory of the humours.[17] Arising from these accounts of woman, a series of problems arise which will be considered in turn here. Is she a monstrous creation? Is she an imperfect version of the male? Does she produce semen, and is this fertile? How is sex determined? What physiological features are unique to woman, and what effects are these thought to have? What are the psychological differences between the sexes?

3.2.1   Is woman a monstrous creation? This question has clear theological associations which have already been discussed above (2.4.1–2.4.3). A monster is something created *praeter naturam*, not in the ordinary course of nature.[18] Although females are the result of a generative event not carried through to its final conclusion according to the Aristotelian theory, sex difference is necessary for the reproduction of the species, and so the female is not monstrous, but is according to the general tendency of nature (*intentio naturae universalis*). A text often invoked is Aristotle's *Metaphysics*, in which it is asserted that men and women are not of different species.[19] Sex difference is a feature of higher animals, but it is postulated in plants and even metals by alchemists, and is essential to mystical understandings of the universe (see above, 2.11.2).

3.2.2   None but satirical or facetious texts support the proposition of monstrosity. They do so often by referring to a sentence in Erasmus's *Praise of Folly*: 'Plato seems to doubt whether woman should be classed with brute beasts or rational beings'.[20] The Platonic text alluded to seems to be *Timaeus* 91A, although this could be applied to men as much as women (see below, 3.7.3). A related Platonic text, sometimes invoked, is from the same section of the *Timaeus*, and suggests that women incarnate the souls of men who in a previous life have behaved in a dissolute or debauched fashion.[21]

3.2.3   It is interesting that so many texts at the end of the sixteenth century contain refutations of this proposition; this may be attributed to the currency of Jacques Cujas's joke (see below, 5.2.1–5.2.4) and the *Disputatio nova contra mulieres* (see above, 2.4.1–2.4.3), which are sometimes confused.[22] The arguments follow the same course: both man and woman are of the same species; sex difference is the material, formal and efficient cause of procreation; woman, in her own sex, is as perfect as man.[23] As the last argument suggests, opponents of Aristotle are able to use the proposition of monstrosity as a means of attacking peripatetic doctors,[24] even though some of the latter refute it as vehemently as Galenists.[25] Wherever monstrous conception and births are discussed, there is little to indicate that woman is considered as such or as responsible for such, except perhaps through the influence of her imagination on the foetus (see below, 3.7.5). It would seem safe to assume that this question was debated only for the sake of form, or to refute a specific satirical text, and that it reflects more on the surprising success of the *facetiae* of Cujas and the author of the *Disputatio nova contra mulieres* than anything else (see below, 6.2.2).

3.3.1   Is woman an imperfect version of the male, and are the anatomical and physiological differences between the sexes caused by a lack of some element or elements in woman? In Aristotelian and Galenic terms,[26] woman is less fully developed than man. Because of lack of heat in generation, her sexual organs have remained internal, she is incomplete, colder and moister in dominant humours, and unable to 'concoct' perfect semen from blood. Two axioms are implied here: that the hottest created thing is the most perfect, and that a direct comparison can be made between the genitalia of man and woman in function, number and form.

3.3.2   A group of peripatetic doctors justify the 'imperfect male' theory by reference to scholastic theology, often specifying Aquinas as the source (see above, 2.2.2); those who distinguish *natura particularis* and

natura universalis in this way include Francisco de Valles (Vallesius)
(1542–92) in a syncretic work entitled *De iis quae scripta sunt physicè in
sacris literis* (1582);[27] Gaspard Bauhin in his *Theatrum anatomicum*
(1592),[28] and Bartholomäus Keckermann (1571?–1608?) in the *Systema
physicum* (1610).[29] Such syncretism is not surprising in followers of
Aristotle, although it is not common to all peripatetics. It is rare among
Galenists, although at least one late example can be cited.[30]

3.3.3   Other physiologists defend the theory of imperfection without
reference to theology. These include Kaspar Hofmann (1574–1648), a
vigorous supporter of Galen and opponent of Harvey. In 1625 he
published a commentary on Galen's *De usu partium corporis* which
includes a general exposition of his views on woman; four years later, in
a polemical work on embryology (see below, 3.4.3), he produces a
coherent account of the axiom of heat and of the differences between
hotter and colder creatures. From this account it becomes evident why
heat is associated with perfection in physical terms. Heat is instrumental
in the production of the most perfectly concocted semen from which the
male will be born, which is produced in the right (hotter) testicle and
deposited in the right (hotter) side of the uterus.[31] The male grows faster
in utero, is of darker and harder flesh, more hirsute, more able to sustain
extremes of temperature, has larger arteries and veins, a deeper voice, is
less prone to disease, more robust, broader, comes to full maturity more
slowly and ages less quickly than the colder female. He may be
ambidextrous whereas she rarely is, and has mental characteristics which
may also be attributed to body heat: courage, liberality, moral strength,
honesty. The female on the other hand, being colder, is characterized by
the deprivation or opposite of these features. The authorities quoted by
Hofmann in establishing these differences based on body temperature
are principally Hippocrates, Galen and Aristotle.[32]

3.3.4   An example of a latter-day orthodox peripatetic is provided by
Cesare Cremonini (1550–1630), in whose polemical treatise *De calido
innato et semine* (1634) is found an apology for Aristotle's theory of sex
difference directed against the Galenists on the specific point of the
efficacy and existence of female semen (see below, 3.4.3). According to
Cremonini, woman is less perfect than man in the context of procreation
(*in ordine ad generationem*), because it is she who carries the foetus and is
the place of conception. Just as the seed is more noble and perfect than
the earth in which it is planted and from which it draws nourishment, so
also is the male more noble and perfect than the female.[33] Both
Hofmann and Cremonini accept the Aristotelian and Galenic argument

that the difference in sexual organs between male and female may be explained by the lack of heat in generation which, in the case of the female, causes the genitalia to remain internal. This leads both to accept comparability of form, number, and general function.

3.3.5   After 1600, the vast majority of doctors reject these axioms in favour of the argument from specific sexual function. Both sexes are needed for reproduction; one sex begets in another, the other in itself, and each has an appropriately differentiated physiology. The earliest suggestion of such an approach is found in the writings of Julius Caesar Scaliger (see below, 3.3.6), although not in a medical context, nor necessarily proposed seriously. A more important influence is Gabriele Falloppio's description of the female genitalia in his *Observationes anatomicae* (1561), which is adduced by many writers,[34] and marks one of the most important changes brought about by experimental anatomy in this domain before 1670. Galen's comparison of male and female genitalia (uterus = inverted penis, ovaries (*testes mulierum*) = testes) is rejected by the *neoterici* in favour of a new alignment drawn from Falloppio (clitoris = penis, nymphae = praeputium, etc.); but although even Falloppio describes male and female genitalia as altogether comparable, it seems that the number, size and function of the specifically compared organs are difficult to establish and, by the end of the sixteenth century, most anatomists abandon this parallelism.[35] The Parisian doctor André Du Laurens writes a very coherent account of this medical dispute in 1593, concluding against comparability;[36] after this, the only asseverations in medical writing which are based on Galenic or Falloppian parallels are to be found in the long debate about female semen (examined below, 3.4.1–3.4.3); it might perhaps be added, however, that Descartes's anatomy makes a Galenic alignment of genitalia.[37] Du Laurens's position, which is that generally accepted after 1600, is consistent with thoroughgoing functionalism, for he rejects also the Aristotelian and Galenic argument of vestigial, non-functional organs in each sex (nipples in man, testes in woman)[38] (see below, 3.4.1–3.4.3). By 1600, in nearly all medical circles, the peripatetic πεπηρωμένον is banished from the textbooks, and one sex is no longer thought to be an imperfect and incomplete version of the other. Indeed, far from being described as an inferior organ, the uterus now evokes admiration and eulogy for its remarkable rôle in procreation.[39]

3.3.6   If woman is no longer an imperfect version of the male, is she yet colder and moister than he? Girolamo Cardano (1501–76) discusses this question as early as 1548 in his *Contradicentia medica*,[40] but it is Julius

Caesar Scaliger's facetious attack on another of Cardano's works, the *De subtilitate*, which gives fresh impetus to the debate. In his *Exercitationes de subtilitate* of 1557, Scaliger sets out to demonstrate that Cardano's inflexible application of the theory of the humours is absurd; in doing this, he claims at one point that man and woman are of equal temperature, but that this is not apparent since woman, being more humid, appears to be colder, and man, the drier, seems to be hotter.[41] Such an argument is somewhat surprising as it comes from a known Aristotelian and anti-feminist,[42] and this may reinforce the suspicion that it is rehearsed paradoxically or as a joke. It is, however, widely quoted by serious doctors as well as feminists.[43]

3.3.7   The debate is made more confused by the fact that not all ancient authorities agree on this point. According to Maurice de la Corde's edition of the Hippocratic (or rather pseudo-Hippocratic) *De morbis mulierum* (1585), it seems that this school of medical thought believes woman's blood to be hotter than the male's, and that she is therefore altogether of a higher temperature.[44] The relevant passage is, however, declared to be an interpolation by Christóbal de Vega (1510?–1573?), the respected professor of medicine at Alcalá de Henares, in his commentary on Hippocrates's *Prognostic* (1552),[45] and most commentators thereafter accept this view.[46] Nearly all other ancient texts can be interpreted to indicate that woman is colder and moister in dominant humours, but after 1580 this is no longer assumed to be a sign of imperfection. Woman's temperature is functional; her colder metabolism causes her to consume ('burn up') food less fast, thus leaving residues of fat and blood which are necessary for the nutriment of the foetus and for the eventual production of milk.[47] When not required for the foetus or newborn child, these residues account for the physiological and anatomical features peculiar to woman (see below, 3.8.1). Such functionalism is, of course, subjacent or even sometimes explicit in ancient texts; but it had become overlaid by the conclusions it had engendered.

3.3.8   While all agree that the hottest male is hotter than the hottest female, it is not clear whether physiologists believe that the hottest female is colder than the coldest male. At least one scholastic source argues this,[48] but Galen in his treatise on the pulse, followed by some late Renaissance commentators, seems to suggest that an overlap is possible, arising from differences of style of life, climate and diet. This might help to account for the ethical problem which arises when some men are dominated by some women (see below, 3.5.2, 4.5.3).[49] That women in general are of lower temperature than men is, however, not questioned, and this has important implications in ethics, in which physiology is invoked to justify the relegation of woman to the home (see below, 4.5.2).

3.3.9   Other conclusions are also drawn from the coldness of woman, which are consistent with Aristotelian and Galenic doctrine, and indeed often explicitly stated in the writings of these authorities. The transfer of this material to the renewed theory of functionalism demonstrates the capacity of Renaissance doctors to salvage from ancient writings whatever details fit into their modified conceptual scheme, and, in using them, still to claim the authority of philosophers whose justificatory structures of thought they have rejected. Menstruation results from woman's colder metabolism; unlike female animals who do not menstruate, she cannot, for sociological reasons (*institutio*) use up excesses of blood in physical exercise, and does not produce bodily hair as does the male. Woman rarely goes bald (that is, 'burns up' her hair). Like boys and eunuchs, she has a high voice, denser, paler, fattier, softer flesh than the male, which burns better than does his on funeral pyres,[50] and is rarely ambidextrous. She takes longer to form in the womb, causes more pain at childbirth to her mother, being less able to help herself than the more active male; but she reaches puberty earlier, and ages more quickly because of the corrupting effect of her dominant humidity. Her physical shape (fatter hips and narrower shoulders than the male) is also the result of colder humours, which do not possess sufficient energy to drive matter up towards the head.[51] The psychological effects of coldness will be examined in greater detail below (4.8.1–4.8.3); it is here that the most obvious dislocation of thought occurs, for it seems that physiologists retain the beliefs in the less perfect mental faculties of woman even after the abandonment of the 'imperfect male' theory: thus Galenists argue not only that woman is equally perfect in her sex as the male is in his, but also that she is inferior to him for physiological reasons.

3.4.1   Closely connected with the debates discussed above is that concerning the existence and efficacy of female semen.[52] The medieval opinion, that woman has testes (what are now known to be ovaries), but that these are residual and not functional, is attractive because of its possible syncretism with Gen. 2:23,[53] and because of its consistency with the dualities male/female, form/matter, act/potency, possession/deprivation. It can also be used as an argument against the enjoyment of coitus by woman, which austere religious moralists sometimes rehearse.[54] Renaissance anatomists expose many Aristotelian and indeed Galenic fallacies about the female genitalia which were authoritative in the Middle Ages,[55] but they have little observational evidence to bring to bear on this topic: indeed, Falloppio even adds some credence to the medieval view by stating in his *Observationes anatomicae* that he was unable to perceive anything resembling semen in the female testes.[56]

3.4.2   Before considering the clash of Galen and Aristotle on this point, it should be said that neoaristotelians of the Renaissance do not even agree as to what really is the opinion of Aristotle. Adelmann points out that this is not surprising, since the *De generatione animalium* is ambiguous on this topic.[57] Prominent among peripatetics who believe that woman has no semen are Julius Caesar Scaliger[58] and Cesare Cremonini;[59] Fortunio Liceti[60] and Joannes Magirus (d. 1596)[61] both represent neoaristotelians who argue that women have semen. To complete a rather confusing picture, one should add that at least one thoroughgoing Galenist, Kaspar Hofmann, argues that women do not have perfect and efficacious semen.[62] There are therefore among neoaristotelians those who declare that woman is imperfect and has no semen (Cremonini); others who argue that although imperfect, woman has a *virtus formatrix* (Liceti); and a third category denying that woman is imperfect or that she lacks semen (Magirus). Similarly, among Galenists, there are those who argue that woman is cold, imperfect and yet has semen (Mundinus Mundinius)[63]; others who argue that woman is cold, but perfect in her sex and possessing a *virtus formatrix* (Du Laurens);[64] and a third category arguing that woman is cold, imperfect and lacks semen (Hofmann). No writer on physiology argues that woman possesses the material and formative faculties sufficient to procreate of herself, although it is argued that the *mola uteri* is a result of the conjunction of woman's (incomplete or imperfect) semen and menstrual blood.[65] One theory not represented above is that of Fabius Pacius of Vicenza (1547–1614), who wrote in his *Commentarius in Galeni libros methodi medendi pars prima* of 1597 that the heat of the uterus is the agent of procreation, and menstrual blood together with semen the matter:[66] this ancient theory had already been refuted by Aristotle, whose arguments are reproduced by Mercuriale against Pacius.[67]

3.4.3   The commonly accepted view is that expressed by Galen in the *De semine* (II.2), which states that woman has semen which is colder and less active than that of the male.[68] The question remains whether it is efficient both formally and materially, or simply materially, or simply formally. The Galenic position, that it contributes to both the form and the matter of the embryo, is that which is most commonly adopted; it helps to explain the resemblance of children to their parents, which Aristotle attributes rather unsatisfactorily to menstrual blood. The rôle of menstrual blood, in both the Aristotelian and Galenic systems, is the provision of matter. This area of medical discussion, which Reinier de Graaf released from obtuseness by his treatise on the female genitalia in 1672, is the subject of a protracted debate involving Mundinius, Parisano, Liceti, Cremonini and Hofmann between 1609 and 1635 in which the orthodox Galenist and Aristotelian positions, the heretical Galenist stance and an uncertain and confused eclecticism (Parisano) are all rehearsed.[69] Although this long debate must appear anachronistic and obscurantist today,[70] it represents nonetheless the last philological enquiry into the subject, and reproduces the most advanced conceptual schemes based on traditional embryology. Modern histories of medicine concentrate on the advances made by experimental anatomists and physiologists (Fabricius ab Aquapendente, William Harvey, Marcello Malpighi), which are indeed important, but more to posterity than to contemporaries. These still relied on a synthetic structure in which Galen and Aristotle are indispensable.

3.5.1   The questions of imperfection and semen are naturally connected with that of sex determination *in utero*. Here a variety of ancient theories known principally through Aristotle's *De generatione animalium* are discussed by Renaissance writers. Sex is said to be determined at the moment of conception by the male semen alone, which may be affected by diet, climate or physical constitution (Aristotle); sex is also said to be determined by the conjunction of male and female semen and their relative temperature (Galen). Another theory, influenced by or influencing Pythagoras's dualities (see above, 1.1.3), attributes sex difference to the position of the foetus in the uterus (left or right side), and the provenance of the semen from the left or right testicle.[71] This last hypothesis is widely commented upon and often found as part of recipes for ensuring that children are of the desired sex (which in nearly all cases is male).[72] Some physiologists, however, doubt it on the grounds of its unprovability.[73] It is clear that most doctors accept the Galenic view of sex determination after 1600.

3.5.2   For those who adopt a coherent Aristotelian position, and for Paracelsus (who in this respect at least resembles an Aristotelian),[74] there is a clear difference between the sexes, and between both sexes and all forms of monstrous (unnatural) births. Among followers of Galen and prearistotelian physiologists, other possibilities are discussed. Whereas, according to Aristotle, sex is a contrariety which does not permit of true intermediaries (since it is based on the opposite of privation), in Aristotle's account of Parmenides's theory, revived by Levinus Lemnius (1505–68), there are two stages of intermediaries between perfect men (the result of dominant male semen and a position in the right-hand side of the uterus) and perfect women (who are born from dominant female semen in the left-hand side of the uterus). These are the effeminate male (dominant male semen, left-hand side of the uterus) and the virago (female semen, right-hand side of uterus);[75] of the latter Felix Platter, Jacques Dubois and Rodrigues de Castro all speak.[76] This does not mean that a perfectly ambiguous creature can be procreated (see below, 3.5.5.); nor does it necessarily imply (although it is sometimes taken to mean this) that the hottest female is hotter than the coldest male. The ranges of humours and temperature are more commonly assumed to overlap, thus providing a rudimentary physiological framework by which ethical and political problems such as dominant wives and successful queens may be explained. An extreme statement of the theory that psychological variations in sex can be attributed to physical constitution is found in the preface to Theodorus Collado's *Adversaria seu commentarii medicinales* of 1615, where it is claimed that all men and women have 'diversae naturae', and that sex has no necessary relation to character (see below, 3.8.3).

3.5.3   Aristotle's account of sex differentiation *in utero* is widely rejected in favour of the Galenic theory by the end of the sixteenth century. This latter theory seems to allow for the production of a sexually ambiguous being, if the temperature of the male and female semen are at a crucial point; it has been seen, however, that a discontinuous spectrum of (normal) sex difference is generally preferred by the Renaissance. This preference may have influenced the debate concerning epigenesis and preformation which emerges from microscope observations in the second half of the seventeenth century. The belief that the individual spermatozoon incorporates a 'preformed' human being reflects the predisposition to find a clear differentiation of sex *ab initio*, which perhaps accounts in part for the popularity of this theory at that time, and the unattractiveness of the theory of epigenesis, although it should be added that this also had impressive adherents, among them William Harvey.[77]

3.5.4   One implication of the Galenist theory which intrigues Renaissance doctors is the question of sex change: there is a *locus classicus* on this topic in Pliny's *Natural History* (VII.4). Whether a woman can

become male is a question related to the debate about the comparability
of male and female genitalia (see above, 3.3.5). The few clinical cases
attested in the Renaissance are all of women changing into men; this is
what would have been expected, as what is perfect is unlikely to change
into that which is less so (even though Ambroise Paré talks of women
'degenerating into men').[78] These cases are all recorded with great
circumspection by physiologists, who prudently do not treat them as
conclusive. Johann Schenck von Grafenberg produces a list of cases in his
Observationes (1584–97) which is subsequently referred to by other
writers on this topic.[79]

3.5.5   Hermaphrodites are also rare occurrences, but are much more
fully documented, notably by Gaspard Bauhin.[80] A possible reason for
the attention they receive is to be found in the importance of the notion
of hermaphrodite or androgyne to occult and neoplatonist currents of
thought in the Renaissance. It is generally agreed that hermaphrodites
belong not at a mid point on the sexual spectrum between (normal)
female and (normal) male births, but rather to the category of monster.
Just as a firm distinction of sex is sought by Renaissance thinkers in
theology and medicine, so also is a firm distinction of natural and
unnatural adhered to (see below, 3.9.3). The causes of monstrous births
(imbalance of blood, semen and heat; illness of one or other parent)
clearly indicate that hermaphrodites belong to the category of
unnatural.[81]

3.6.1   Next to be considered are the unique physiological features of
woman which are relevant to her general notion.[82] Menstruation is one
of these. In the Middle Ages this was firmly associated with the
malediction (Gen. 3 : 16), with uncleanness, and with certain deleterious
physical effects, usually relating to the transmission of diseases (notably
smallpox) by heredity or contagion. The malignity of menses is
chronicled in ancient medical texts, notably in Aristotle, Columella,
Pliny and Plutarch[83] and these opinions are reproduced by early
Renaissance writers.[84] A debate on this topic occurs, in which Jean
Fernel (1497–1558) and Jean Riolan the Elder (d. 1606) support the view
that menses are malignant in a variety of ways,[85] whereas later writers,
Bottoni, Mercuriale and Rodrigues de Castro, all argue that menses are
only malignant when the whole female organism is ill.[86] It is true that
some doctors argue that they possess curative powers or virtue, but
closer examination of the texts reveals that these powers are attributed to
them because of the sympathy between the disease and the menses,
which far from being beneficial are in this system as noxious as the

disease on which they act homeopathically.[87] For all this, there is far less stress on the noxious nature of menses at the end of the sixteenth century, and the majority of texts stress their harmless excremental nature. In doing so, they can be said to contrast with neoscholastic theological texts, in which the paradigm clean/unclean is upheld. There is, as might be expected, an abundant clinical literature on this subject.

3.7.1   A series of questions about the uterus, raised in antiquity and debated in the Renaissance, is also of interest here. Is the uterus an animal in its own right, endowed with powers of movement and a sense of smell? Is it eager to procreate (*avidum generandi*)? What ill-nesses does it cause in woman? Is it sympathetic to the moon and the imagination?

3.7.2   The conflicting ancient texts concerning the animality of the uterus are those of Plato (*Timaeus* 91A) where the uterus is described as a ' καθάπερ τι ζῷον παιδοποιίας ἐπιθυμητικὸν ' (*animal avidum generandi*) and Galen, who refutes the Platonic view that the uterus is animal because of its alleged powers of independent movement and its alleged sense of smell in several texts, notably the *De locis affectis* (IV.5). Galen accounts for the movement of the uterus by claiming it is caused by the constriction or relaxation of muscles, and dismisses the alleged sense of smell as ridiculous. Early Renaissance anatomists consider the Platonic doctrine as a sort of metaphor, and pour scorn on the anatomical description of the uterus by Galen; this tentative sympathy for Platonic anatomy is taken up not only by certain doctors, including Jean Riolan the Elder, but also in popular literature by François Rabelais.[88] The overwhelming majority of physiologists seem, however, to accept Galen's criticism of Plato on this point, and refutations of the view that the uterus is an independent being living in woman may be found in many writings.[89]

3.7.3   A second question is whether the uterus makes woman eager to procreate, and desire the male. Such a view accords well with the Aristotelian concept by which the imperfect should desire the perfect: the comparison is found in *Physics* 1.9 [192a 22]: 'matter desires form as the female the male'. The jurist André Tiraqueau throws doubt on the reading of this passage,[90] but he seems to be alone in the Renaissance in doing so; certainly Falloppio accepted the authority of the text as quoted here (see Chap. 3, n. 14). This argument is rehearsed by Riolan the Elder,[91] it is also reflected in Bonacciuoli's etymology of vulva from *volens*.[92] Scaliger, however, asserts in his *Exercitationes* (CXXXI.4) that the sexes desire each other mutually, and that no argument about perfection or imperfection can be made about the uterus's alleged avidity for coitus. The fact of mutual desire has, of course, never been in doubt psychologically; for this reason, perhaps, there is no late defence of this proposition. It is even enshrined in the *locus classicus* (*Timaeus* 91A–D) in which Plato refers to the unruly member in man which is equivalent to the uterus.

3.7.4   Women are sometimes said to be more prone to illness than men;[93] this is nearly always attributed to the influence of the uterus.[94] The etymological association of hysteria with ὑστέρα (=uterus) is well known; many of its forms are psychological. Even woman's garrulity (see above, 2.7.2) is said to be one effect of hysteria;[95] *furor uterinus*, or excessive desire for coitus, is another which attracts much comment.[96] Mercado has an exhaustive list of hysterical illnesses, many of them inducing lovesickness, melancholia, listlessness and irrational behaviour.[97] This is evidently one reason why women are thought to possess weaker powers of mind compared to men, but there is no clear agreement as to which powers are in question. Another cause of irrationality cited is the supposed singularity of cranial suture (*sutura sagittalis*) in woman, which does not allow humours to escape and hence subjects their brains to 'perturbationes' (passions).[98] Thus although many of these doctors argue that woman is as perfect in her sex as is man in his, they do not accord to her equal possibilities for psychological control.

3.7.5   Two external forces are said to act on the uterus: the moon and the imagination. Most doctors record the ancient belief in the influence of the moon; Du Laurens doubts this, although there is little sign that his hesitation is known to many outside the anatomical sphere.[99] The alleged effect of the imagination (the 'power to generate mental images') on the uterus, especially during pregnancy, causing birthmarks and deformities, is also noted.[100] Paracelsus and other occult philosophers make much of this.[101] Some doctors comment on this belief; its most comprehensive refutation does not occur until 1727, written by J. A. Blondel (*The strength of imagination in pregnant women examined; and the opinion that marks and deformities arise from thence demonstrated to be a vulgar error*). It seems still to hold some credence in the popular mind today.

3.8.1   For the Renaissance, the physical characteristics of woman exclusive to their sex – colder and moister humours, menstruation, the womb and its diseases – have psychological implications. There are *loci classici* in which these are recorded: the most celebrated of these is found in the *Historia animalium* IX.1 [608a 21ff]:

In all genera in which the distinction of male and female is found, Nature makes a similar differentiation in the mental characteristics of the sexes. This differentiation is the most obvious in the case of human kind and in that of the larger animals and the viviparous quadrupeds. In the case of these latter, the female is softer in character, is the sooner tamed, admits more readily of caressing, is more apt in the way of learning . . .   In all cases, excepting those of the bear and leopard, the female is less spirited than the male, . . . softer in disposition, more mischievous, less simple, more impulsive, and more attentive to the nurture of the young; the male, on the other hand, is more spirited than the female, more savage, more simple and less cunning . . . the nature of man is most rounded off and complete, and consequently in man the qualities or capacities above referred to are found in their perfection. Hence woman is more compassionate than man, more easily moved to tears, at the same time is more jealous, more querulous, more apt to scold and to strike. She is, furthermore, more prone to despondency and less hopeful than the man, more void of shame or self-respect, more false of speech, more deceptive, and of more retentive memory. She is also more wakeful, more shrinking, more difficult to rouse to action, and requires a smaller quantity of nutriment.

3.8.2   This *locus* is not exhaustive, nor is it necessarily systematic. Its scientific basis is the theory which relates bodily humours to mental characteristics; a combination of cold and moist produces a retentive memory because, like wax, impressions can be registered easily and remain fixed on cold and moist substances. The memory, which is sometimes described as 'intellectus passibilis' (see above, 2.5.1), is also associated with woman (*vs* man) as is passive (*vs* active) (see above, 2.2.1). Imagination is thought to be stronger in woman because cold and moist objects are subject to metamorphosis; another form of metamorphosis is found in mental changeability, manifesting itself in deceit, inconstancy, lack of stamina, infidelity, but also inventiveness.[102] Many inventions are traditionally associated with women in popular literature. The effect of the uterus on the mind weakens rationality and increases the incidence and violence of passions in women: hate, vengeance, fear, anger are all thought commonly to hold greater sway over the female sex; but also compassion, pity and love.[103] The softer flesh of woman predisposes her to psychological softness (*mollities*), which is described as a vice or defect in the *Nicomachean Ethics* (see below, 4.3.5); childbirth predisposes her to a greater tolerance of pain.[104] Such psychological assumptions are not systematized in the writings of either Aristotle or Galen, although the latter gives some indication of the relationship between the humours and psychology in the *De humoribus*. They are present in authoritative texts often in the form of incidental remarks; perhaps for this reason orthodox medical writings tend to make less reference to them than popular literature. Galen himself, after demonstrating the influence of extraneous factors (style of life, diet, climate) on humours in the male and the female, suggests that medical students should be careful to relate humours to their whole context (*totius rei naturam*).[105] By using Galen's example of a misleading case, Julius Caesar Scaliger is able to ridicule the inflexible application of the theory of the humours to psychology in his *Exercitationes* (CCLXXIV). Other arguments about sexual psychology based on physical phenomena are also attacked in the Renaissance; an example is the proof of natural modesty (*verecundia*) in woman – the fact that drowned female corpses float face downwards in the water – which is discredited by Bonacciuoli, and shown to result from purely anatomical causes.[106]

3.8.3   Some doctors, notably Martinus Akakia and Rodrigues de Castro, assert with vehemence that women are equal to men in the *operationes animi*, just as they are the equal of men in the perfection of their sex.[107] This argument has theological weight. Jerome asserts that sex is not of the mind [*animus*],[108] and Aquinas's argument that sex is not of the soul [*anima*] is similar, although not explicitly identical.[109] The operations of the mind referred to seem to be those associated with the image of God understood as *anima rationalis*: will, intellect and memory (see above, 2.5.1). This conflicts with the popular notion of woman's psychology (3.8.2) which makes her inferior in the first two operations and superior in the last. Another suggestion is made by Theodorus Collado, who puts forward the theory of a random distribution of mental strengths and weaknesses in both sexes.[110] There seems to be little support for this hypothesis, as might be expected, for it undermines both the difference of sex, which is an indispensable duality in Renaissance as in scholastic thought, and the theory of the humours, which is the dominant theory of psychological difference. Even to those doctors who argue that woman is equally perfect in her sex as is man in his, the fact of her coldness is accepted and with it the psychological implications mentioned above. Moreover, the psychological effects of the uterus are not denied by such doctors, who accept also that the 'passiones animi' can in turn affect the uterus, inducing sterility.[111] It is clear that psychological limitations must have a bearing on the ethical status of woman; her assumed frailty of body, which best befits her for the care of the young and makes her unsuited to exposure to the dangers of the outside world, is accompanied by mental and emotional weaknesses which are the natural justification for her exclusion from public life, responsibility and moral fulfilment.

3.9.1   From this discussion of medical commentaries and texts, it emerges that the Aristotelian notion of woman is abandoned by 1600 by most doctors in favour of a modified form of Galenism, in which some elements of the Aristotelian synthesis remain, and some tenets of Galenism are adapted to concord with the results of new anatomical studies and clinical observation. This eclectic approach leads to attempts to remove ambiguities and conflicting opinions in ancient authoritative writings. The popularity of the title *Contradicentia medica* is testimony to this, as well as indicating an underlying desire for synthesis and a continuing respect for ancient medical philosophy. While real advances are being made by patient observation and experiment in narrowly defined areas of study, the vast body of Renaissance medicine is struggling to maintain a synthetic outlook with the help of ingenious but sometimes makeshift strategies of interpretation.

3.9.2   By the end of the sixteenth century, many doctors are convinced that the notion of woman has changed, and that by the removal of the taint of imperfection she has attained a new dignity. But although she is thought to be equally perfect in her sex, she does not seem to achieve complete parity with man, or does so only at the expense of considerable dislocation in medical thought. Her physiology and humours seem to destine her to be the inferior of man, both physically and mentally; the doctors who argue that she is his equal in the *operationes animi* are either inconsistent with the general context of medical science to which they adhere in most cases, or, more rarely, have Paracelsian tendencies, as does Theodorus Collado. Woman, therefore, remains notionally the inferior of the male.

3.9.3   Two aspects of Aristotelian thought reinforce this notion of inferiority. The first is the metaphorical association of woman with mother earth, nutrition, fruitfulness and the fluctuations of the moon, which is deeply embedded in the substratum of ancient medical thought, and sometimes explicit there.[112] The implications of these metaphors – passivity, receptiveness, compassion, mutability – may account in part for the Renaissance view of female psychology. The second aspect is the primordial nature of sex difference. Sex difference is not only a feature of the higher animals; it is postulated in plants and stones. The difference is an example of the opposite of privation (the 'species privata': see above, 1.1.4). Even after the arguments which make the female a deprived form of the male have been rejected, the *difference* of sex retains the associations of deprivation, and plays an important part in the infrastructure of Renaissance thought.

3.9.4   As well as bearing comparison in the 'species privata', woman is also compared with man in the 'species relativa'. To this potential source of confusion must be added the presence of prearistotelian dualities (left/right, even/odd, male/female etc.) which are sometimes culled from Aristotle himself, and sometimes quoted from texts of the Hippocratic corpus. Empirical data certainly cast doubts on these Pythagorean opposites, as does the revised understanding of functionalism, developed by Renaissance thinkers in a way which parallels the development of mechanism;[113] but they remain present in some degree in nearly all late Renaissance medical texts. They operate under the aegis of the pre-eminent duality of natural/unnatural. The force of this duality has been apparent throughout this chapter, but its exact sense is hard to define. It includes not only that which is part of nature, constituting a criterion of 'the natural', but also that which belongs to the process of nature defined by the Aristotelian da Monte as 'principium motus et quietis corporum naturalium'.[114] This definition implies intention or plan; Aristotle is eager to show purpose to be inherent in nature.[115] More powerful still than the *intentio naturae* (which Christian philosophers might wish to understand as 'the tendency of nature') is necessity: 'many things occur by natural necessity which are not part of nature's plan' declares the peripatetic aphorism.[116] Woman, in Aristotelian terms, is part of the general plan of nature, which effects procreation by the conjunction of the sexes; she is *necessarily* born female, because of the prevailing conditions at the moment of her conception. But as an individual, she is not planned by nature, whose *intention* is always to produce the most perfect being. By arguing that woman is 'equally perfect in her own sex' as the male is in his, late Renaissance Galenists resolve this anomaly, and thereby disunite the physiology and anatomy of male and female in matters of sex. The argument of 'equal perfection' marks thus a transition from the 'species privata' to a version of the 'species relativa', in which factors external to sex (temperature, physical and mental powers) promote comparisons. But this 'species relativa' still incorporates the notion of purpose in nature and the notion of hierarchy; and both still work to the disadvantage of woman's status *vis-à-vis* man.

3.9.5   One important factor which acts as a liberating force on medical philosophy is the absence of the paradigm of marriage. This is very influential in theology and, like the opposite clean/unclean, is one which belongs to the 'species contraria immediata' (see above, 2.11.3). Unfettered by these paradigms, Renaissance physiologists can conceive of a continuum rather than fixed states; in their eyes, all mankind is in a process of continual change linked to age and health; but in this process woman changes more, and more often, and within a shorter space of time.[117] Medical writers can proclaim that they have raised the status of woman in declaring her to be equally perfect in her sex; in removing from her physiological functions the taint of uncleanness; in describing her in terms which take account of the continuous change to which she is subject. It might even be claimed that the impressive bibliography of works concerning gynaecology and gynaecological diseases between 1540 and 1600 is some indication that more attention is being paid to the special problems of the female sex. For all this, woman is considered to be inferior to man in that the psychological effects of her cold and moist humours throw doubt on her control of her emotions and her rationality; furthermore, her less robust physique predisposes her, it is thought, to a more protected and less prominent rôle in the household and in society. Although apparently not bound by the authority of the divine institution of matrimony, doctors nonetheless produce a 'natural' justification for woman's relegation to the home and exclusion from public office, and provide thereby, as well as coherence with a central tenet of theology, an important foundation on which arguments in ethics, politics and law are based.

4

Ethics, politics, social writings

4.1.1 Any discussion of ethics and its related disciplines in the Renaissance is made difficult by the profusion of relevant texts, and the critical questions to which they give rise. Is there a European tradition of commentary-writing? Is this, if it exists at all, continuous from Aquinas to the seventeenth century? Is it possible to detect the influence of social, political and economic forces in commentaries – in other words, do the Reformation, the variety of forms of government in Europe, contemporary examples of female rule and economic activity by women affect the exegesis? Do Renaissance scholars attempt to see woman as described by Aristotle in historical or sociological terms? To what degree are commentaries affected by new textual discoveries, textual emendation and the study of the Greek as well as the Latin text? What is the relationship between contemporary political and moral philosophy (Machiavelli, Bodin, Montaigne, Vives) and the commentaries of Aristotle's works? To what degree does the content of the commentary vary according to the intended readership and pedagogical demands? It may not be possible in the confines of this investigation to provide satisfactory answers to all, if any, of these questions, but they should be borne in mind, as they form the critical basis of this enquiry.

4.1.2 The practice of producing expositions, commentaries and scholia as adjuncts to the ethical, political and 'economic'[1] texts of Aristotle is medieval in origin; indeed, Aquinas's commentaries are still known and quoted with respect in the seventeenth century.[2] Expositions and commentaries are very common in the Renaissance, especially after the publication of the Aldine Aristotle (1495–8) and the emergence of new texts in the Aristotelian corpus, notably the third book of the spurious *Economics*.[3] One may account for the great number of commentaries on the *Nicomachean Ethics* as much by its presence on university curricula as by its use as a means of disseminating moral philosophy more widely. This is a general pedagogical preoccupation which is reflected also in the vulgarization of ancient texts on ethics. Not only do these appear in the vernacular, but also humanists such as Erasmus and Vives popularize them in works intended to reach as wide an audience as possible (the *Enchiridion militis Christiani* (1504), the *De institutione foeminae Christianae* (1523), etc.). In doing this, they ensure that the moral lessons of the ancients are translated into a Christian context. The same may be said to be true to a lesser degree of commentaries on classical political writings; these are to some extent superceded by contemporary writings on political topics which have a greater air of immediacy through their reaction to and reflection of current events.

4.1.3   Most of the commonplaces considered here are Aristotelian in origin, and reflect in their vocabulary the method and terminology which underpins all Aristotelian philosophy: genus, differentia, species, act, potency, form, matter and so on. This poses complex linguistic problems, as A. H. T. Levi has shown, when the words used in Aristotelian ethics (*virtus, ratio, voluntas, affectus, prudentia*, etc.) are transposed into neoplatonist or neostoic contexts.[4] Plato and Aristotle will be seen to be in conflict on more than one occasion in this chapter (see below, 4.2.1, 4.4.3); the degree to which this conflict is real, or only the result of Renaissance formulations, is a question beyond the scope of this enquiry. For the sake of convenience, this chapter begins with an account of 'practical philosophy' and its divisions and hierarchy; then moral philosophy, 'economics' and politics are considered in turn in relation to sex difference. The chapter ends with the question of intellectual virtue and woman.

4.2.1   'Practical philosophy' is traditionally divided into three parts: Ethics (the good of the individual *qua* individual), 'Economics' (the individual's happiness in relation to domestic affairs) and Politics (the good of the state, and of the individual in relation to the state). There are ancient debates about the precedence of these disciplines, recorded by Renaissance commentators. Plato describes 'economics' and politics as the same discipline, different only in scale,[5] whereas Aristotle, followed by Plutarch, gives precedence to 'economics' because the household comes before the state, both in proximity to nature and in historical formation.[6] Such a view makes the male a natural master, which has important implications in 'economics', as will be seen. Some Renaissance writers argue that 'coming before' does not bestow seniority, only greater age on the science of 'economics', which, in their view, should be considered as part of political philosophy as in the

Platonic view;[7] orthodox neoaristotelians insist on the peripatetic hierarchy.[8] All are agreed that ethics precedes both disciplines.

4.2.2   Ethics is to a large degree the study of virtue, which is either moral·or intellectual (*Nicomachean Ethics*, 1.13, II.1 [1103*a* 4ff]). Moral philosophy, which will first be examined, is distinct from moral theology in important ways: the end of the latter is spiritual good (*bonum spirituale*), whereas it is moral good (*bonum morale*) in the case of the former;[9] furthermore, at least in Aristotelian terms, the capacity for moral virtue (and hence the nature of the mean) varies from one class of individual to another, and from one age to another in a normal life span (*Politics*, 1.13 [1260*a* 20ff], *Nicomachean Ethics*, II.6 [1105*a* 24ff], VII.7 [1150*b* 12f], IV.1 [1121*b* 14] etc.); whereas in moral theology, virtue and vice are categories which are not discussed in terms of human diversity or change. It is clear also that the issue of moral responsibility and guilt looms much larger in moral theology. These differences underlie the similarities which cause theologians of the Renaissance to quote Aristotle's *Economics* and Plutarch's *Conjugalia praecepta* in support of St Paul or Proverbs (see above, 2.9.1), and humanists to attempt the syncretism of ancient wisdom and Christianity. Conflicting views on points of detail can of course be found,[10] but in general discrepancies are noted less than similarities.

4.2.3   In the context of practical philosophy, man is a complex being, with a multiplicity of rôles and functions, sometimes private, sometimes public, sometimes master, sometimes subject. Historical moment, social conditions and conventions, sex, age, climate, diet all affect one's moral and political being. The variations in individuals and in the conduct most suited to them derive from such factors as these; sex is but one of them. In ancient moral philosophy it attracts very little direct comment, and much of what follows is inferred or extrapolated from authoritative texts by Renaissance commentators, rather than being explicit in them.

4.3.1   At the base of all practical philosophy, according to most sects, is the virtue of prudence (*prudentia*),[11] which rules the will and appetites of the individual (ethics), or the individual in relation to a greater number ('economics', politics). One commentator asks whether prudence is present in equal measure in all human beings, and concludes not, as both the humours (*temperamentum, complexio, humores*) and experience make older men (being cold and dry) more prudent than younger men, and the male in general more prudent than the female.[12] It seems that both Plato and Aristotle agree on this point.[13] Now prudence, according to Aristotle, belongs especially to the person who commands (*imperans*),[14]

and this authority (*imperium*) can derive either from convention, as with
tyranny or monarchy, or from nature, as is the case with man's authority
over woman; the male is *naturally* more robust, more rational, less
subject to fluctuating emotions (see above, 3.8.1–3.8.3). It is habitual for
commentators to refer to *Nicomachean Ethics*, VIII.10 [1160b 21ff], where
it is implied that the wife's subjection to her husband, like the child's
subjection to his father, derives from nature.[15]

4.3.2   This natural authority is reflected in man's ability to arrive at
measured and well-reasoned decisions; his deliberate faculty or
judgement (*consilium*) is sound. In *Politics*, I.13 [1260a 11], Aristotle refers
to the judgement of men, women, slaves and children: only men have
full powers of judgement, for slaves (or servants) lack judgement
because of their status,[16] children have imperfect (though perfectible, in
the case of male children) judgement, and women possess 'consilium
invalidum et instabile' (this is the most commonly encountered Latin
formulation for βουλευτικόν ἄκυρον) because of their temperament and
imperfection. This commonplace is widely quoted.[17] In the case of
women, slaves and children, the lack of judgement arises from a natural
or conventional state which does not bring the individual into conflict
with himself; but in man, it can lead to the paradox of an individual at
once dominant in the household and obedient to the will of another or
others as a citizen.

4.3.3   This conflict is most thoroughly investigated by the Ferrarese
Antonio Montecatini in his *In politica progymnasmata* of 1587. His
resolution of the problem owes much to two Aristotelian *loci*, *Politics*,
I.13 [1260a 20ff] and *Nicomachean Ethics*, I.7 [1098a 17]. The good master
of the household who is also a good citizen possesses two sets of virtues,
one for commanding and one for obeying. In both perfection is possible.
The difference between these sets of virtues is not one of genus but of
species: Montecatini amplifies species to 'ratio et modus' which might
be rendered as 'raison d'être' and 'mode' or 'external form'. The
paterfamilias-civis is not therefore in conflict with himself, but fulfils in
different ways contrary functions by the exercise of the same generic
virtue.[18] Other commentators approach this paradox by quoting
another Aristotelian *locus* (*Nicomachean Ethics*, VIII.12 [1162a 16ff]), in
which man is said to be by nature more a conjugal than a political
animal.[19] Thus by nature man is dominant in the household, by
convention obedient in the state. The importance of these arguments
will emerge when the inherent moral conflicts in woman are examined
(see below, 4.3.6, 4.6.6).

4.3.4   Does woman have any capacity for moral virtue? The preconditions seem to be a capacity for prudence, judgement and authority, or the free exercise of the will (*Nicomachean Ethics*, III.2 [1111*b* 4ff]). Whether or not woman possesses prudence depends on the nature of this virtue, which is an active state of character or habit (*habitus*), as opposed to a faculty or a passion. We have already seen that woman is associated with the passive and man with the active: this also is a commonplace, deriving from *De anima*, III.5 [430*a* 21]. It would seem that, by the associations of passivity and the female, and activity and virtue, woman is excluded from all moral behaviour. Yet, on at least one occasion, Aristotle explicitly states that woman is able to act morally (see below, 4.4.3).

4.3.5   One area which seems to remain uncontradictory is that of 'imperfect virtue' (*Nicomachean Ethics*, IV.9 [1128*b* 10ff], VII.7 [1150*a* 30ff esp. 1150*b* 15]). When the vice of 'softness' (*mollities*) is discussed, Aristotle provides one of his rare mentions of woman in the *Ethics*. Renaissance commentators, extrapolating from the text, point out that *mollities* (the defect of endurance) is not always voluntary, and hence not always a vice. In woman, old men and those living in inclement climates it is a natural state.[20] The natural leaning of woman to *mollities* (a word often said to be cognate with *mulier*)[21] suggests that the imperfect virtues of *continentia*, *verecundia* and *tolerantia* which are 'more like feelings than states of character' (*Nicomachean Ethics*, IV.9 [1128*b* 10]), may also be associated with her,[22] and it is indeed striking that chastity, modesty and long-suffering are closely identified with the female sex, even by stoic writers.[23] Woman, by her association with passivity, seems excluded from Aristotle's moral universe, unless she obtains entrance through these virtues deemed as imperfect as she is thought to be.

4.3.6   Renaissance commentators approach this problem in several ways. Francesco Robortello (1516–67), writing in 1552, declares that either nature, or habit, or education makes men good, but they are limited in potency by their *habitudo corporis*, which seems to be another way of referring to the humours.[24] If this is the case, woman is placed at a great disadvantage to her male counterpart, since she has a tendency to vice, less impulsion to virtue because of weaker powers of reason and judgement, and is furthermore subjected to the 'natural' state of marriage, in which the wife 'must bend her will to the will and authority of her husband, and follow his advice in all decent things'.[25] The suggestion that the wife has no will of her own had been extended by the early humanist Francesco Filelfi (1398–1481) to apply to all women, whom he denies are moral creatures.[26] The less severe Montecatini, using the model of the *paterfamilias-civis* (see above, 4.3.3) sets out the reasons why woman can act morally within the terms of her natural obedience to husband (or, presumably, guardian) in a memorable exposition. Woman possesses the virtues of temperance, liberality, justice and all others but of a different class (*species*) and in a different way (*modus*) from man. Her rôle in life causes them to be expressed differently: the same perfection of virtue is possible to the person who must obey, if it is appropriately adapted ('quantum convenit parenti'). Furthermore, the measure (*mediocritas*) of the perfection of a virtue is the individual practising the virtue: thus woman, although less robust physically and mentally than the male, is able to practise virtue as perfectly as he.[27] In arguing thus, Montecatini postulates the existence of a 'deep structure' in which male and female virtue are identical (the contention of Socrates and for Plato); this deep structure then undergoes transformations which can result in contrary surface manifestations (obedience:command; silence:eloquence). This union of apparently contradictory ancient doctrines (see below, 4.4.3) marks him to be a late example of a committed syncretist (cf. below, 4.8.1).

4.3.7   Montecatini's stance may be compared to that of a 'feminist' doctor in the favour it shows, within an Aristotelian context, to woman. Other neoaristotelians are less generous. Klemens Timpler, writing in 1610, seems to allow for moral action by woman when he indicates that a distinction should be drawn between those human beings who use their reason and those who do not; 'neither infants, nor idiots, nor madmen, nor irrational creatures, insofar as they are irrational, can act morally'.[28] Woman may not possess rational powers as great as those of man, but even their *consilium invalidum et instabile* leaves room for some exercise of reason, and so, grudgingly, woman is given some sort of precarious place in a moral universe.

4.3.8   At the same time, woman remains subject to man, and her will is not free. The justification of this subjection in pagan writing is to be found in the different physiques and psychologies of the sexes, which Renaissance writers on ethics and politics repeat; to this is added the malediction of Eve, reinforcing natural with divine law.[29] The most that can be accorded to woman is an imperfect moral existence, if complete consistency with peripatetic teaching is sought. This is characterized by Theodor Zwinger (1543–83), who coins the phrase 'prudentia economica' (domestic prudence) to describe this restricted virtue.[30] The limitation on the freedom of the will which this implies throws into doubt Montecatini's assertion that there is a difference only of species between the moral acts of man and of woman.

4.4.1　　Is the nature of virtue in man and woman then different, and do different virtues apply to each sex? Before attempting to elucidate Renaissance attitudes to this ancient debate, the linguistic problem which underlies it should first be considered. In commentaries on the *Nicomachean Ethics*, the words *vir* and *homo* are used almost indiscriminately, perhaps reflecting the usage in the parent text of ἀνθρωπος and ἀνήρ. It is not clear what to make of this, for even when writing of the male alone, Renaissance authors sometimes lapse into using *homo*, perhaps under the influence of the vernacular (cf. below, 5.2.2). For this reason it would seem unwise to associate the wayward usage of these words with the debates about the humanity of woman (see above, 2.4.2, and below, 5.2.1).

4.4.2　　On the other hand there is striking usage of the epithets *virilis, muliebris, effeminatus*. It is discussed at length by the jurist André Tiraqueau (1479–1558),[31] and can be exemplified by Seneca's statement 'anger is a womanly [and childish] vice' ('ira est vitium muliebre [et puerile]', *De ira*, 1.16); I bracket the last two words, because they are not always quoted with the rest. If they are quoted, then the use of epithets suggests that the cold and moist humours which women and children have in common are responsible for the defect or vice of anger. Such a statement implies that virtues and vices have a foundation in the individual's temperament, which we have seen to be implicit also in Galenic and Aristotelian medicine and the *Nicomachean Ethics* (see above, 3.8.1, 4.3.5).[32] When stripped of the addition 'et puerile', Seneca's statement can be interpreted as an association of conventional characteristics of gender (which may arise from sociological causes, or even simply reflect prejudice) with the physical fact of sex. Thus it would be possible to talk of 'women with manly virtue' (see above, 2.11.2) not necessarily as a paradox, nor as an indication of a monstrous exception (the *virago*), but as a means of drawing attention to the psychological qualities of the women in question and suggesting at the same time no necessary connection between 'manliness' and 'maleness', 'effeminacy' and 'femaleness'.[33] Such a usage is found in the description of nations as 'soft and effeminate' or 'strong and virile'. It is even embodied in the traditional etymology of *virtus* from *vir*[34] (cf. below, 5.2.3). One may sense here the same dislocation of thought which underlies the assertion that woman's *operationes animi* are equal to those of the male (see above, 3.8.3).

4.4.3   A well-known set of *loci classici* is available to Renaissance commentators on this topic. Plutarch's moral essay, the *Mulierum virtutes*, had assembled some of these in antiquity; he begins with the differing opinions of Thucydides and Gorgias before arguing that male and female virtue is identical by citing famous historical examples of heroic acts performed by women. Before him Plato (*Republic*, v; *Laws*, vii, *Meno*, 71–5) and Aristotle (*Politics*, 1.13 [1260*a* 20ff]; *Economics*, 1.3 [1344*b* 30ff]) discuss the issue, and their widely known views are often simplified into a debate between Socrates/Plato who argues (at one point) that no distinction should be made between male and female virtue, and Aristotle, who clearly distinguishes the two:

The temperance of a man and of a woman are not, as Socrates maintained, the same; the courage of a man is shown in commanding, of a woman in obeying ... And this holds of all other virtues, as will be more clearly seen if we look at them in detail, for those who say generally that virtue consists in a good disposition of the soul, or in doing rightly, or the like, only deceive themselves. Far better than such definitions is the mode of speaking of those, who, like Gorgias, enumerate the virtues. All classes must be deemed to have their special attributes; as the poet says of women
                    'Silence is a woman's glory'
but this is not equally the glory of man. . . . (*Politics*, 1.13 [1260*a* 20])
A man would be thought to be a coward if he had no more courage than a courageous woman, and a woman would be thought loquacious if she imposed no more restraint on her conversations than the good man. (*Politics*, iii.4 [1227*b* 20])

Here Aristotle argues both that virtue is a function of the individual and his natural capacities and limitations; and also that virtue *in genere* is an unprofitable approach to this topic. A confusion may arise here, for it is possible to extrapolate from Aristotle's text two lists of virtues which are not so much species of the same virtue as contraries or opposites of the 'species contraria immediata' which are consistent with the opposition of sex: viz.

           male   female
      eloquence   silence
      command   obedience [. . .]

These are not dissimilar to Pythagorean dualities (see above, 1.1.3), although, unlike them, they are susceptible of justification in the 'natural' association of male–eloquence–command, etc. It will be seen how this is developed in the anomalous case of the princess (see below, 4.6.4–4.6.7). It is also possible to infer from this text, as does Montecatini, that virtues are different only in scale or mode of expression and that the same virtue can have contrary manifestations.

4.4.4   Before considering Renaissance reactions to these conflicting views, a word should be said about stoic and neostoic arguments on this topic. It is sometimes said that stoicism made no distinction between the virtues of man and woman, but urged both to aspire to virtue by effort and to practise apathy and *constantia*. The ancient evidence for this is equivocal; it is true that Epictetus and Seneca both use common nouns (ἄνθρωπος, *homo*) and adjectival nouns to describe the stoic *sapiens*, but there is also a tendency (noted above in the case of Seneca) to distinguish 'masculine' and 'feminine' virtue on the grounds of strength and weakness, and the one direct reference to women in Epictetus's *Enchiridion* (LXII) exhorts them to practise the traditional female virtues of modesty and respectfulness. The neostoic writers of the late sixteenth century (notably Justus Lipsius (1547–1606) and Guillaume Du Vair (1556–1621)) continue to use common nouns, and also make the distinction between male and female, and that between virile and effeminate, parallel to that between strong and weak. Furthermore, they also insist on prudence as the moral virtue *par excellence*, and express this in terms of masculine political functions (prince, magistrate, citizen).[35] The general impression left by these writings is that, if woman is exhorted to practise the stoic virtues, it is within the context of her domestic rôle or function: that is, by apathy and patience in suffering.

4.4.5   There are broadly three Renaissance reactions to the conflict of views set out above. The first, which is neoplatonist or neostoic in inspiration, claims that man and woman have an identical capacity for virtue, and should practise identical virtues. Such a reaction is found in feminist writing;[36] it is sometimes qualified by the assertion that woman's different domestic and social function imposes on her the practice of certain virtues not required in man (modesty, silence) and releases her from the need to cultivate others which relate especially to man's rôle in society and the household (courage, eloquence). Here woman is liberated from her subordinate ethical place in relation to man, but at the same time refused the opportunity of practising the traditional heroic virtues of courage, liberality and magnificence. A similar strategy is adopted by enlightened social commentators such as Baldassare Castiglione (*Il cortegiano*, 1528) and Nicholas Faret (*L'honnête homme*, 1630), who legislate for the new Renaissance phenomenon of the court. These writers claim for women equal virtue; but at the same time they affirm the social conventions which give to women simultaneously the benefits of deference and the disadvantages of legal and marital subservience. This suggests that they combine a conservative desire to maintain the fabric of society as it is with a radical reappraisal of woman's capacity for virtue. This inconsistency is perhaps common to all social and political thinkers who claim (perhaps even with sincerity) that all they wish to do is to propose the alteration of one element in society or politics without causing the general context to change, even though it is clear that this must undergo modification if any one element which goes to make it up is itself modified. But this strategy of argument may reflect also no more than lip-service to the enhancement of the status of woman, and conservatism for its own sake, perhaps justified by a fear of the effects of social change.[37] As an intellectual position, it is neither in harmony with a coherent Aristotelian view, nor with Galenic medicine.

4.4.6   The second reaction is that characterized by Montecatini (see above, 4.3.6); here the notion of the identity of male and female virtue *in genere* is retained as a deep structure, but subjected to a transformation which produces different *officia* (duties) in relation to society and to the individual. These *officia* are said to result from the different physiological and social functions of the sexes. Woman needs to be protected from public life as she is the instrument of procreation, and in her the future of mankind rests. The virtues she must practise are distinct not *in genere*, but *in ratione et modo*; it is thus incumbent on both sexes to be just, temperate, continent, courageous, and so on, but in relation to their function. Such functionalism is paralleled by that of enlightened Galenist doctors (see above, 3.3.5). It is not clear how, if at all, such ideas can be adapted to theories of social change.

4.4.7   The third reaction is represented by commentators who argue that male and female capacity for virtue *in genere* is different, and that they should practise different virtues which are often complementary in character (silence, eloquence; obedience, command). This view is embraced by those who see as the source of all female virtue *prudentia economica*, such as Theodor Zwinger. It finds favour with syncretic writers on moral philosophy such as Erasmus, Agrippa and Vives, all of whom wish to see no change in woman's position in society, whose institutions are divinely ordained. They retain not only woman's theological subordination to man, but also an area of Christian responsibility (see above, 2.9.2). When writing in contexts other than moralistic literature, humanists such as Erasmus argue that customs can be changed to allow, for example, for women to be learned;[38] but they

do not seem to want to abandon the divine ordering of household and
society which severely restricts woman's moral horizons.[39]

4.5.1   Having considered woman's relation to moral virtue *in abstracto*,
we may next turn to her place in 'economics' or the household. The
mulier economica is essentially a woman married, about to be married,
destined for marriage or a widow: there is no place in the system of
practical philosophy for the woman who intends to remain unmarried,
nor indeed, as the Calvinist Klemens Timpler points out, is virginity a
moral virtue.[40] His opinion may, however, be seen as religiously biased,
and to some degree comes into conflict with the mystical doctrine that
virginity is a gift of God, and a 'virtue' at least in the sense of 'power' (see
above, 2.11.3). The belief that woman cannot be considered except in
relation to the paradigm of marriage is reinforced by the ethical and
medical vision of marriage as a natural state, found even in animals who
possess neither a deliberative faculty nor freedom of choice.[41] Because
Renaissance commentators on ethics consider matrimony in relation to
nature rather than to divine law, they are able to ask such questions as the
relative naturalness of polygamy, polyandry, polygyny, monogamy
and the community of wives without incensing religious opinion.
Indeed, the disagreement of Plato and Aristotle over the question of the
community of wives attracts much commentary.[42] Whereas marriage
in Christian terms has mystical associations which add to its dignity,[43] in
pagan writings it is no more than a natural state, the 'imago civitatis',
and the bond of the household.

4.5.2   In marriage, the rôles (*officia*) of man and wife are different, and
this is often ascribed to the differing physical and mental attributes of the
sexes. Man, more robust and audacious, is better suited for a peripatetic,
outdoor, public, acquisitive rôle; woman, more timid, possessing
judgement and physical force in lesser measure, is naturally the custodian
of children, household goods and the acquisitions of her husband
(*Economics*, 1.3 [1343*b* 27ff]). This division is sometimes accentuated by
the use of a 'double comparative' (in the 'species relativa'): man is
robustior, *nobilior*, *audacior*, woman *infirmior*, *ignobilior*, *timidior*. This can
be compared to the less vigorous form of the comparative found, for
example, in the Pauline epistles (e.g. 1 Cor. 7:8–9). It is not clear
whether this is merely a verbal habit of Renaissance commentators, or a
deliberate stylistic feature used to highlight the gap in proficiency and
strength between the sexes and emphasize their opposition.[44] Woman's
private existence in the home also prevents her from exciting
concupiscence by public appearances: religious moralists are emphatic

on this point.[45] The argument that virtuous women deserve public fame, rehearsed in Plutarch's essay *Mulierum virtutes*, conflicts with this view, but does not provoke commentary from Renaissance writers. The heroic exploits of exceptional women are noted, but moralists do not advise emulation of them, but rather their translation into domestic and private terms.[46]

4.5.3   As women are different from men in robustness and intellect, so also do men and women differ from others of the same sex. Now it is possible to conceive of the strongest and most rational female being stronger and more rational than the weakest and least rational male: we have encountered this theoretical overlap before (see above, 3.3.8). If a marriage were to take place between such persons, then either the wrong person or the wrong sex would command. One commentator (Juan Gines Sepúlveda (1491–1571)) examines this hypothetical case and concludes that it would be unnatural for such a marriage to occur, but that if it did, the *officia* of husband and wife would follow temperament and not sex.[47] One may suspect here, as with legal problems concerning the right to succession of hermaphrodites (see below, 5.3.1), a piece of amusing casuistry rather than a serious critical point. A similar case, that of a rich wife dominating a poor husband, is quoted by Joannes Magirus as an example of oligarchic society, and also condemned as unnatural.[48]

4.5.4   There are undisputed commonplaces about woman and her place in the household. Aristotle's insistence that it is barbarous to fail to distinguish women and slaves, who have manifestly different *officia* (*Politics*, 1.1 [1252b 1ff]) is widely quoted, and sometimes reinforced by historical examples.[49] The same philosopher's statement that man must rule his slaves like a tyrant, his children like a king and his wife like a politician (*Politics*, 1.12 [1259a 37ff]) is also well known, and usually linked with the three states of *consilium* in woman, children and slaves (see above, 4.3.2).[50] By political rule, Renaissance commentators understand the seeking of advice, which is then not necessarily heeded. It is assumed that, of all members of the household, women are the most difficult to govern.[51] In both *Politics* and *Economics*, Aristotle places woman immediately below her husband in the domestic hierarchy.

4.5.5   The duties of woman in the household are set out most clearly in the spurious third book of the *Economics*, which is frequently quoted by moralists of the Renaissance. The wife should subject her will to that of her husband, look after his property, keep strangers out of his house, be modest in personal habits and dress, be tolerant of her husband's moods and behaviour, and pray for him in his absence.[52] Such advice, which is embodied also in Plutarch's *Conjugalia praecepta*, accords well with Judaeo-Christian teaching. The chaste, modest, silent, submissive, hard-working, soberly dressed, pious and longsuffering wife emerges as the model of Juan Luis Vives's seminal moralistic work *De institutione foeminae Christianae* (1523). Such works, which are impregnated with a distrust of woman's weak nature and her propensity to evil and to sinful passions, appear if anything more repressive than pagan texts on this topic.[53]

4.5.6   The nature of the emotional relationship between wife and husband is also of interest here. The need for reciprocal love and respect is everywhere stressed: by love is meant not passionate attachment, but something akin to an amalgam of Christian charity and the virtues of chastity and endurance (*tolerantia*). The English neoaristotelian John Case goes further than this, and perhaps referring to *Nicomachean Ethics*, VIII.12 [1162*a* 16], declares that a wife should also be a friend.[54] Other commentators recall that Eve was created to be a helpmeet for Adam (*adjutorium simile sibi*: Gen. 2: 18) and place the same high value on conjugal love.[55] It is also common, however, to find passages in Renaissance moralistic literature which throw doubt on woman's capacity for true friendship.[56] Conjugal love is different for husband, who is enjoined to respect an inferior, and wife, from whom obedience is expected.[57]

4.5.7   One last aspect of the *mulier economica* deserves mention. As has been pointed out, her place in the household is immediately below its head, the *paterfamilias*, and above children and slaves. As such she exercises power in the administration of the household, but although possessing authority she must act in accordance with the general wishes and desires of her husband. Renaissance commentators are explicit on this point.[58] There is no problem where the slaves are concerned, but the control of children is 'principally in the hands of the *paterfamilias*'.[59] Some commentators suggest that it is natural for the mother to have the care of the education of daughters, and for the father to see to that of sons. Vives suggests that it is the mother's duty to be involved in the religious education of all children.[60] As for authority over the careers and marriages of offspring, it is clear from formulae in customary law ('les père et mère') that woman has this to some degree, but no reference is made by commentators or moralists to such power, unless it is to decry it.[61] The *mulier economica* is therefore a person of limited actions and powers doing 'suitable tasks' (*labores honestae*) and administering the household in her own right, but within the guidelines laid down by her husband: her 'economic' rôle, like her moral rôle, is limited, private and overshadowed by the male.

4.6.1   We may now turn to the question of woman in relation to politics. As well as the reactions provoked by contemporary political events, there are debates centred on ancient commonplaces on this topic. These are taken from Plato, Plutarch and Aristotle.[62] One of the ancient examples of female intervention in public life is Sparta; Aristotle's discussion of this (*Politics*, II.9 [1269b 12ff]) points to the economically destructive lust of women for riches and luxury, their licentiousness and its debilitating effect on the morals and discipline of warriors, and claims that their involvement in politics at all is unnatural.[63] A related commonplace, also popular in the Renaissance, is taken from Plutarch's Life of Cato the Elder (VIII), in which Cato is reported to have said 'In all nations, men command women; we Romans command all nations, and women command us', referring to the insidious influence of women in the state.[64] As might be expected, the Aristotelian position attracts more sympathetic commentary than Socrates's theoretical statement in Plato's *Republic* that women should participate equally in the running of the state; it is noteworthy that the arguments of Socrates's adversaries are cited as authority, as well as his own, by Renaissance writers.[65]

4.6.2   Both in commentary on these commonplaces, and in implicit or explicit reference to contemporary examples, there is near unanimity in the distaste shown for the notion of woman's involvement in politics. Nature and convention, divine and human law all predispose man rather than woman to govern, and if woman is to be involved in public life, it should only be in emergency or because the woman in question possesses outstanding qualities of leadership. Such a point of view is supported by theological, medical, ethical and 'economic' authority, as we have seen. The syncretic nature of Aristotelianism emerges clearly in the arguments rehearsed by Renaissance commentators on this subject, many of whom marshall commonplaces drawn from all these disciplines to support their exclusion of women from public life.[66] Such lengthy expositions indicate the vehemence of conservative reaction to such political figures as Catherine de Médicis, Mary Queen of Scots and Elizabeth I.[67]

4.6.3   There are examples of neoaristotelians who attempt to justify the prominence enjoyed by some women in affairs of state. One example is the Oxford scholar John Case, whose *Sphaera civitatis* of 1588 has a feminist frontispiece portraying Elizabeth I as a sphere encompassing the qualities of majesty, prudence, courage, religion, clemency, eloquence and plenty. It is not surprising that he argues eloquently in favour of female rule after such a liminary emblem. Aristotle's declaration that the perfection of masculine virtue is in commanding, and that of feminine virtue in obedience must not, according to Case, be interpreted to mean that some women are not suited to command, but rather 'women in general' are not suited to command. Furthermore, he argues, this statement relates to 'economics' and not to politics; other commentators also make this point, and add that by divine law the wife shall be subservient to the husband, but not to all men.[68] After setting aside the imperfect judgement of women (see above, 4.3.2) as relating only to wives, Case concludes:

Nature often makes woman shrewd, hard work makes her learned, upbringing makes her pious, and experience makes her wise. What, therefore, prevents women from playing a full part in public affairs? If one is born free, why should she obey? If one is heiress to a kingdom, why should she not reign? Divine law, the history of nations, ancient institutions, and examples drawn from Holy Writ all support such arguments.[69]

The relationship of the humours to mental powers is also considered by Case, who argues that humours always affect the body but not always the mind. This, and the examples of successful female administration which he adduces (which include Sparta) make his orthodoxy as an Aristotelian, on this topic at least, very precarious. Case mentions in passing the question of whether woman should be allowed to wage war; this is considered by other Renaissance commentators, who adduce the arguments rehearsed above, and conclude for the most part that she should not.[70]

4.6.4   A specific problem arises over the moral and political activities of princesses, or women closely associated by marriage or blood to the throne. A ruler is required to practise virtues which are in some sense contrary to those recommended to woman in general (see above, 4.3.1); how then should queens, princesses and other women who by their social status form part of public life, behave? Various answers are suggested by Renaissance theorists. Agostino Nifo (1473–1538) considers ancient declarations on this subject in a section of his *De principe*, and notes that ancient noblewomen were praised for chastity, conjugal fidelity, stoic apathy, patriotism, learning and eloquence, political activity and liberality. He then considers the virtues recommended to women in general: moderation, modesty, chastity, temperance, abstinence, sobriety and silence. These concord quite well with those he has already established to be the virtues of a ruler:

prudence, justice, modesty, mildness, piety, humanity. Thus, for him, there is no great problem in recommending the wives and daughters of rulers to behave like their husbands and fathers.[71]

4.6.5   Torquato Tasso's *Discorso della virtù feminile e donnesca* of 1582 presents the topic as contentious, and sets out to resolve it. According to Tasso, each sex has a dominant virtue, one which both sexes need to practise, but which is more important to one than to the other. The dominant virtue is chastity in the case of women, and courage in the case of men. The dominant vice for each sex becomes the antithesis of the dominant virtue (lack of chastity, cowardice), and the most excusable vice the antithesis of the dominant virtue of the other sex. Thus for men it is most unforgivable to be cowardly, and most forgivable to be unchaste; for women the vice of *impudicitia* is most to be abhorred, and cowardice the least reprehensible vice. Chastity and courage are seen, therefore, in some sense as contrary virtues when placed in a sexual context. Tasso goes further, and attributes some virtues to men and some to women, producing thereby a kind of sexual ethics (cf. above, 4.4.3). Men may be virtuous in practising eloquence, liberality, courage, magnificence; women by being silent, economical, chaste, modest. The implication is that it is inappropriate for a woman to be eloquent and liberal, or for a man to be economical and silent, although not, of course, unvirtuous. Public honour is also more suitable to a man than a woman.[72]

4.6.6   Tasso then encounters a problem in his discussion: what if moral duties clash with political duties? What if, as a royal person, one is encouraged to be eloquent, liberal, magnificent, and as a woman economical, silent and modest? This problem leads to a discussion of the relationship between moral and political virtues; the practice of the former, argues Tasso, leads to personal happiness, and the practice of the latter, to the proper functioning of the state. The moral virtues assigned to woman are suitable to a member of the bourgeoisie or lesser nobility; they do not appear to be so to a princess, who is enjoined by her royal status to practise the heroic virtues. Tasso argues that the first duty of a princess is to her royal status; it is therefore forgivable, though regrettable, if she neglects her moral virtues such as chastity in the pursuit of her royal virtues, as was the case with historical figures such as Semiramis and Cleopatra. The princess is, as it were, a man by virtue of her birth, and hence the masculine standard of morality applies to her. The difference between the sexes is therefore subjugated to the social or conventional expectations which, according to Tasso, regulate moral behaviour. It is clear that such an argument was bound to attract refutation.[73]

4.6.7   In Tasso's discussion of the virtue of princesses, and in Case's arguments about female rulers, one may detect an unspoken hesitation about the women in question: are they exceptional, or do they indicate latent qualities in their sex as a whole? If they are considered to be exceptional, then the infrastructure of Aristotelian thought remains intact; if they indicate qualities latent in all women, then the physiological basis of ethics (see above, 3.8.1) must be rejected, and with it some theological justifications for the subordination of women. A further, practical, problem arises if this second solution is chosen: should society remain as it is, or should it be modified to recognize the latent qualities in women? As in the case of moral virtue (see above, 4.4.5) dislocations of thought occur. A clear example is to be found in feminist works which first argue the equality of male and female virtue by citing the examples of women who, for their acts, have achieved public fame and honour; but then translate these examples into domestic terms, use them to encourage women to be chaste, obedient, thrifty, silent and so on.[74]

4.6.8   It may well be asked why, if women possessed latent qualities unrecognized in their social dispensation, they tolerated their fate for so long. Among the explanations for this might be cited the strength of such institutions as marriage with its legal, theological and ethical associations; the lack of education for all women except those who were already emancipated from the disqualifications suffered by the mass of their sex, such as the high-born; and possibly also the fact that women possessed greater freedom, independence and power than is generally recognized. This last suggestion might account for the attribution to women of influence and political intriguing as wives or sisters of kings, mistresses and court ladies; and for the revulsion shown by religious moralists for such influence.[75]

4.7.1   All that has been discussed so far concerns active, moral virtue; we may now turn to the question of intellectual virtue and its relation to women. This problem is not specifically discussed in Aristotle, and the few classical *loci* are all in the form of specific examples of intellectual virtue in women (Diotima, Sappho, Cornelia, etc.). Intellectual virtue, whose end is truth, relates to speculative reason, and there seems in the Renaissance to be little support for the incursion of women into this sphere. There are, of course, many notable examples of learned women in Italy, France and England, but these were either involved in literature as poets or novelists, or known for their erudition which they did not exercise publicly. One of the few women to talk in metaphysical terms was the sister of François I, Marguerite de Navarre, who was criticized by the following generation of moralists for her utterances in this sphere.[76] Such criticism may appear somewhat surprising, since woman was accorded, in the hermetic and neoplatonist tradition in the Renaissance, a pedagogical and mystical rôle (see above, 2.11.4). There are indeed famous female mystics in the Renaissance, but few, if any, mathematicians, cosmologers, or theologians. This is perhaps connected with the limited educational facilities available to women, but it also reinforces the beliefs current in the Renaissance about woman's more limited powers of reason. Women are associated with a privation of meditative powers (*contemplationis defectus*) which makes them, with rustics and the simple-minded, well suited to devoutness, but ill suited to intellectual disciplines.[77] No effort is made, outside the highest court spheres and 'eccentric' humanistic families, to remedy this privation. The education conceived for girls is different from that of their brothers, and its substance is in the main morally edifying. A late sixteenth-century French writer who produced a handbook of logic for his daughters admonished them only to practise this among themselves, because 'the use of destructive argument (*elenchi*) with your husbands is too dangerous', presumably for the 'correct' hierarchy of marriage.[78] Even such education as is allowed by quite enlightened moralists to women is secondary to their training in humdrum domestic duties; the fruits of learning should only be enjoyed when these are completed, and should not supplant traditional female pastimes of spinning, weaving, embroidery and so on.

4.7.2   One sphere in which women were counselled to display their learning was at court. The court lady as described by Baldassare Castiglione in Book 3 of *Il cortegiano* must have all the accomplishments required to sustain conversation in civilized company; her very position in such society runs counter to the strictures applied to her as a moral, domestic and intellectual being. The *taciturnitas* for which the domestic woman is praised is abandoned; her private exclusive relationship to a dominating husband is replaced by a public, promiscuous, social rôle in which, by convention, she is the dominant partner; she is splendidly arrayed, in spite of moralists' warnings about the feminine weakness for vanity, ornament, extravagance and luxury; she enjoys the delights of food, music and dancing despite her supposed propensity to sensuality.

4.7.3   This mode of life conflicts not only with ancient prescriptions but also with Christian moral teaching. It raises to some degree the question of the double standard of morality, which relates most obviously to adultery (see above, 2.7.1) but also is implicit in social freedom. It is to be expected that moralists in a patrilinear and patriarchal society would recommend a private and domestic rôle for women as wives, and reject social and marital liberty for both sexes except in the case of courtesans. The 'Querelle des amyes' in France in the 1540s adumbrates this issue, and examines the court lady from various points of view. The outstanding contribution is that of Antoine Héroet (*La parfaicte amye*), in which the plight of the unhappily married woman and her relationship to her courtly lover are portrayed. Neoplatonist doctrines of love are here much in evidence, as they are in Castiglione's treatise, and justify the presence of women at court, both because of their beauty and because of their virtue.[79]

4.7.4   Below the social level of the court, it seems to be assumed by moralists that the rules of conduct which pertain to women are those of the *mulier economica*. The spirit of the austere writings of Church Fathers on female propensity to sin and to indolence breathes through even the tracts of enlightened humanists like Agrippa, Vives and Erasmus. If time cannot be spent in continuous household tasks or spinning, sewing and embroidery, they recommend only edifying reading and denounce novels and poetry.[80] Yet Erasmus, in one of his *Colloquia* ('abbatis et eruditae') seems to be suggesting that learning might be a solution to the problem of leisure among women of the middle classes. In France at least, it is the path by which, through the writings of St Francis of Sales and later Jacques Du Bosc, women eventually formulate their own ideal of social behaviour, the *précieuse*, who is less elevated than the court lady but aspires to the intellectual and marital freedoms which she enjoys.[81]

4.8.1   The topic of woman, learning and social behaviour in Renaissance Europe has been exhaustively investigated by Ruth Kelso, whose extensive bibliography indicates its great importance in the moralistic literature of the period. The same can be said to be true of the topic of gynaecocracy, which is a burning issue in France, England and Scotland in the middle of the sixteenth century and provokes much scholarly debate and polemic. On the other hand, the more theoretical question of woman's place in the universe of ethics evinces few specific discussions; this may be because it was taken for granted that woman as well as man is in question in ethics; it is also possible that she is tacitly excluded because of her psychological disadvantages and lack of freedom of action in the confines of the 'natural' society of marriage.

One may detect a slight shift of emphasis in interpretations of Aristotle made in the late sixteenth century, but the room for manoeuvre is small. This shift is most notable in Montecatini's writings, and probably reflects both the influence of neoplatonism in his thought and his attempt to harmonize the teachings of Plato and Aristotle.[82]

4.8.2   In all practical philosophy, the female sex is considered in the context of the paradigm of marriage. It is the bridge by which syncretism is made with Judaeo-Christian writings, which add their authority to that of ancient moral philosophy. Marriage is subjected to much examination and discussion in the Renaissance, but it is difficult to see more than minor shifts of emphasis occurring, principally connected with the husband's rôle and function. Historical and comparative studies of the institution begin to appear in the latter part of the period,[83] but they rarely suggest that it is subject to radical change. One of the most frank discussions of marriage is to be found in Montaigne's essay 'Sur des vers de Virgile', but this prudently does not recommend any modifications.[84] The earliest debates about trial marriage, divorce, and the abolition of the institution in a Christian context of which I know are to be found in John Milton and in the conversations of *précieuse* women as recorded by Michel de Pure in the 1650s; it is true to say, however, that polygamy had been discussed much earlier.[85] As in theology, marriage is one of the strongest barriers to conceptual change concerning the status of woman.

4.8.3   The idea of sex difference in ethics is consistent with that found in Aristotelian and Galenic medicine. It incorporates both the opposite of privation and that of relation (see above, 4.3.2, 4.5.2). In common, also, with medical studies, ethics and politics reflect the renewed interest in functionalism (see above, 4.4.6). Woman's protected and conservative rôle in the household and in society is justified by arguments from naturally preordained function, as is the institution of marriage itself. These structures of thought make changes in the realm of moral philosophy very difficult without dislocations of a fundamental nature. Such dislocations do occur: they are caused by changes in society such as the activities of queens, queen regents and court ladies, and the emergence of a class of women possessing leisure and the aspiration to fill it profitably. Claims that women have equal virtue and mental powers and an equal right to education become more strident throughout Europe after the middle of the sixteenth century.[86] This implies that the physiological justification for the subordination of woman is ignored or rejected, creating both dislocations within practical philosophy and inconsistencies with other disciplines. Scholastic faculty psychology had incorporated aspects of physiology and the science of the humours; by the late Renaissance, the link between psychology and temperament is no longer so well defined, at least in so far as woman is concerned. It may be suggested also that Aristotle's delineation of vices and virtues, timeless for scholastic commentators, is beginning to seem antiquarian to late Renaissance readers. The growth of such historical feeling is, however, more evident in studies on Roman Law, as will be seen in the next chapter.

5

Law

5.1.1 The primary focus of this investigation is on commentaries connected with academic disiplines; of these law is among the most wide ranging. No attempt is made here to survey systematically this vast field of study; such an undertaking is far beyond the limited scope of this enquiry. Nor will there be any systematic attempt to relate the theoretical status of woman to that which she actually enjoyed. Much work remains to be done in this area, although there exists a useful collection of essays, published under the auspices of the Société Jean Bodin in 1959 and 1962.[1] It is hoped nonetheless that the inter-disciplinary nature of the notion of woman and its ramifications in law will emerge from the very brief survey undertaken here.

5.1.2 Nearly all faculties of law on the continent of Europe in the later Middle Ages and Renaissance concern themselves with Civil and Canon Law. The great medieval Italian school is strongly influential from the fourteenth century onwards; it is associated with the names of Accursius, Bartolus and Baldus. Its method – the 'mos italicus' – led less to philological accuracy or historical truth than to an unhistorical interrelationship of all manner of law, and to a use of the interpretative methods of contemporary theology. This method was succeeded – although not eradicated – by the 'mos gallicus', which has its origins in Italy in the work of Lorenzo Valla (c. 1406–57), but is developed in France by Guillaume Budé (1468–1540), Andrea Alciato (1492–1550) and their pupils. The 'mos gallicus' separates Roman Law (the Corpus Juris Civilis) from contemporary European law, makes of the former a wholly academic pursuit, and by the use of increasingly sophisticated philological methods, develops an awareness of historical change which was in turn to transform the study of customary law and feudal law, and play a decisive rôle in the development of historicism and historical writing.[2] By the middle of the sixteenth century, the study of Roman Law concentrated on the expurgation of gloss, interpolation and anachronism from the text. The 'mos italicus', however, survives, and is made available by extensive republication (e.g. the *Tractatus iuris universi* of 1584, which runs to twenty-seven folio volumes); it is still invoked by German schools of law in the seventeenth century.

5.1.3   The expurgatory approach of the humanistic jurists suppressed, except in rare cases, the infrastructure of jurisprudential reasoning and explanation which is explicit in the 'mos italicus'. The medieval Italian school of law sought to create a coherent framework for legal discourse by juxtaposing legal texts and by drawing justification and elucidation from theological, medical and ethical writings. For this reason, it provides more material for our purposes than the 'mos gallicus'. Even early humanistic jurists such as Giovanni Nevizzano (d. 1540) and André Tiraqueau quote widely and freely conclusions or commonplaces drawn from other disciplines, and this practice is continued in some legal writings throughout the sixteenth century. The converse – Roman Law cited by theologians – is also true, and testifies to the deep-rooted desire for synthesis characteristic of the scholastics.

5.1.4   There is in Renaissance legal writings a surface similarity which to some extent derives from the division given in *Institutes*, 1.2.12: 'all law pertains either to persons, or to things (*res*),[3] or to actions'. This division was not unchallenged in the Renaissance,[4] but it goes far to account for similar disposition of material in texts which could not possibly have influenced each other. The habit of the 'mos italicus' of dialectical presentation (usually the case to be refuted is presented first), lingers on also in many of these texts, recalling the deep imprint left by scholastic thought and method on the intellectual infrastructure of the Renaissance.

5.1.5   The most rigorous humanistic jurists, eschewing the rather accumulative and unselective practice of the 'mos italicus', concentrate on the establishment of the original texts of Roman Law and on the elimination of *antinomiae*. These legal contradictions were sometimes resolved by the claim that there had been interpolation in the text, sometimes by philological methods. Attention was paid especially to the linguistic features of legal texts by means of analogy with 'pure' classical Latin and by means of etymology. The medieval interest in opposition, description and definition as a means of elucidating the meaning of a text recedes, although it is clearly still present in the work of early humanistic jurists such as Nevizzano and Tiraqueau, and is naturally in question when sex difference, fundamental to much law, is discussed.

5.1.6   One of the major points of difference between the medieval and humanistic approaches to law lies indeed in the attitude to language, exemplified in Alciato's influential essay and commentary on *Digest*, 50.16.1 *De verborum significatione*. Here the validity of the scholastic method of definition by *genus*, *species*, *propria* and *differentia* is thrown into doubt, and a method is preferred which looks for the 'spirit' (*voluntas*) of an utterance (that is, the intention of the speaker) by a study of *proprietas*, usage and past interpretations.[5] The application of a theory of words which tends to link them to fixed meanings and postulates a moment in the past at which a language was static and coherent (a moment which can ideally be recreated by patient study[6]) can be exposed to ridicule, even by other humanists; Jacques Cujas's joke on the word *mulier* is an example of an intelligent jurist's awareness of the shortcomings embodied in an inflexible philological approach. Cujas's joke will be examined first in this chapter, because it provokes reactions which indicate well the nature of woman in the eyes of jurists. After this, the following questions will be considered: what constitutes sex difference, and how does it relate to other differences recognized by law (marital, social, functional and so on)? in what does woman's *deterior conditio* (*Digest*, 1.5.9) lie? in what ways is she the equal of man? in what ways is she his superior, and for what reasons?

5.2.1   Is woman a human being? This question, which arises in theology (see above, 2.4.2) and medicine (see above, 3.2.2), is also asked by jurists. It is connected with the interpretation of words such as *masculus*, *mulier*, *femina*, *homo*, *si quis*, *quicunque*, and appears first in the Renaissance in assertions that woman is not a monster.[7] In the latter part of the sixteenth century, Jacques Cujas (1522–90), one of the greatest of French humanistic jurists, produced a flippant gloss on the Roman law of homicide (*lex Cornelia de sicariis*) in his *Observationes et emendationes* (1587) which achieved considerable notoriety:

The Roman emperors considered infanticide to be punishable by death: the murderer of a man was punished in the same way. The law therefore pursued homicide with an avenging sword. It was possible to doubt whether the law covered the murder of infants, as the *lex Cornelia* says 'who kills a human being (*homo*)', hence the name of the crime (homicide) . . . in the same way it was possible to doubt whether the murder of a woman is covered by the law. Now an infant is not a human being; nor, properly speaking, is a woman (see the passage 'quis aliquid' § abortionis in the section *De poenis* of the *Digest*). But in the *lex Julia et Papia* the meaning of 'human being' is extended by the jurists, as in the *lex Cornelia*, to include 'woman' too.[8]

The offending words to subsequent jurists seem to have been 'woman, properly speaking, is not a human being' ('femina item non proprie est homo'). A similar gloss, also flippant, is produced at about the same time by the German jurist Scipio Gentilis (1563–1616), who declares himself that his interpretation of the passage in the *De poenis* (*Digest*, 48.19.38) is intended to be a joke.[9] This Cujas does not do, but it is clear to at least one seventeenth-century reader (Gerard Vossius) that it is.[10] Contemporaries, however, assume the text to be serious, and link – or even confuse – Cujas with the author of the equally satirical *Disputatio nova contra mulieres* (see above, 2.4.2), even though he was dead at the time of the appearance of this tract.[11]

5.2.2   There are several refutations of Cujas: the most cogent and detailed is that of Johannes Goeddaeus (1555–1632) in his commentary on the *De verborum significatione* (1604), which is evoked respectfully by subsequent writers.[12] Goeddaeus sets out to establish as an axiom that 'the female sex is included in the male sex [in the law of homicide] not only thanks to an extension of meaning but also in the proper signification [*proprietas*] of the word'. He cites many legal texts, and biblical and classical *loci*, to establish that woman is a human being, and that, although inferior to the male, she is his equal in humanity because 'a smaller or greater quantity of a thing does not entail a specific difference or form, but only distinguishes the thing by quantity or quality'.[13] As well as refuting Cujas by rejecting the medical argument of woman's non-humanity (see above, 3.2.2), he provides an alternative interpretation of the passage in the *De poenis* to which Cujas refers. This speaks of those who administer love philtres and draughts to provoke abortion, and states that they are punished by death 'si eo mulier aut homo perierit'. Where Cujas (flippantly) interprets this to mean that 'mulier' must be excluded from the category 'homo', Goeddaeus states that 'mulier' appears in this context because to her alone can a 'poculum abortionis' be administered, whereas a 'poculum amatorium' can be administered to either sex ('homo').[14] Another explanation of this passage is offered by Joachimus Eberartus in 1616, in which the 'poculum abortionis' alone is in question, and 'homo' refers to the embryo, which can be either male or female.[15] No-one seems to have considered the possibility that a casual error, or a lax formulation, has been made here, either in Roman times or by a subsequent copyist.

Goeddaeus concludes this section of his commentary with a reference to another passage from the *De verborum significatione* (*Gaius de lege Julia et Papia*, 50.16.152) 'there is no doubt that both woman and man are included in the appelation *homo*'. 'Masculus' and 'femina' or 'mulier' are not interchangeable terms, but both belong to the genus *homo*, and there is an area of common ground shared by both; so much emerges from Goeddaeus's own analysis of the puzzling passage of the *De poenis*.

5.2.3   One path to the specific meaning of a word is its etymology: it is frequently said that *mulier* derives from *mollicia*, *femina* from *femur* (which is a metaphor for lust), 'woman' from 'woe unto man' or 'with man', *vir* from *vis* or *virtus*.[16] This interest in etymology and sense is strongly reminiscent of Plato's *Cratylus*, which Renaissance commentators read as a serious treatise on names.[17] Philological study of words is also in evidence: *mulier* is thought by Valla to refer only to a married woman, by analogy with Cicero, although most jurists assume both *mulier* and *femina* to include *virgines viripotentes*, married women and widows alike.[18] There are, of course, common nouns and formulae (*si quis*, *quicunque*) as well as those relating to one or other sex, and even *masculus* and *femina* can sometimes comprise the whole of humanity. The anonymous *Lawes resolutions of women's rights* (1632) provides a copious list of such terms: 'heretic, traitor, homicide, felon, parricide, cutpurse, rogue, foeffor, foeffee, donor, donoree, vendor, vendoree, recognisor, recognisoree'.[19] Such common nouns are of course subject to contextual restriction; that is, even if the formulation is common (*si quis*), it may exclude woman if it refers to a function she cannot exercise (magistrate, coroner, bishop, abbot), or an action she cannot commit (rape, forced marriage).[20]

5.2.4   It is interesting to note that Goeddaeus accepts woman's inferiority to man, but rejects the argument of imperfection. He reflects thereby the position of Galenist doctors, who reject the doctrine of *mas occasionatus*, but accept psychological distinctions which are disadvantageous to woman. In Canon Law, woman's physiology, as well as her psychology, is reflected in the dispensation which is made for her. Mosaic law relating to uncleanness (see above, 2.7.5) is translated into prohibition to enter certain churches and monasteries and into acts of purification.[21] In mental attributes, woman is characterized in Canon and Civil Law alike by 'lunata levitas', 'inconstantia mentis' and 'consilii incertitudo et imbecillitas'.[22] Thus in Renaissance legal tracts, the same underlying association of physical and mental weakness in the female sex can be detected as is in evidence in theology, medicine and ethics.

5.3.1   Even if the nature of woman is not generically different from that of man, there is, as has been seen, a difference between the sexes. The law does not recognize an intermediate stage between man and woman, male and female; hermaphrodites are to be classed with the sex which they resemble the more (*Digest*, 1.5.10). This principle seems to have passed without alteration into feudal law. One may suspect of legal flippancy the commentator who speculates on succession in a family of hermaphrodites and daughters:[23] such theoretical considerations indicate, as does Cujas's joke, a playful attitude to the more ponderous aspects of an academic discipline.

5.3.2   The area in which sex difference *per se* has the greatest effect is in succession to kingdom, title or property. The concept of the individual in law is to some extent inseparable from implications of title, property and function; by depriving the female sex of certain sorts of succession, jurists are restricting her existence as a legal individual. The question of women and succession has great antiquity. In the twelve tables of ancient Roman Law, difference of sex seems to have not been considered in establishing succession, but the *lex Voconia* imposed a sexual disqualification in inheritance laws after the Second Punic War (218–201 B.C.). This law was repealed under Justinian in the sixth century, allegedly at the instance of his wife, Theodora.[24] The history of this change in Roman Law is recorded in the Renaissance by François Baudouin (1520–73) in 1559, to whose account jurists refer with respect.[25]

5.3.3   Two aspects of laws of inheritance preoccupy Renaissance jurists: Salic Law, which concerns the succession to the crown of France, and feudal succession. There is a copious literature on the first topic in the second half of the sixteenth century more because of its national and sectarian implications than because of its disqualification of women. Donald Kelley has shown the importance and complexity of this topic in late Renaissance legal thought.[26] An extensive examination is beyond the scope of this enquiry; for our purposes, the account given by Denis Godefroy (1549–1622) of the arguments for and against female succession to kingdoms in his *Praxis civilis* of 1591 is a sufficient indication of the co-ordinates of the discussion. He produces twenty-one reasons in favour of female rule, beginning with theological and natural arguments of equality, before passing in review historical and comparative, public and private, canon and civil, statute and customary law in order to establish the principle of sex equality in succession. He ends the thesis by stating that if the reasons which justify any prohibition have been shown to be invalid, then the prohibition itself should be discarded. The 'antithesis' – the case in favour of Salic Law – comprises six arguments. The first is a justification from nature and custom of woman's exclusion from public life, which answers the opening argument of the 'thesis'. After this, the legal points made in the 'thesis' are answered both technically and by reference to *raisons d'état*. Succession to kingdoms is not in the gift of kings, but is vested in divine and human law; just as women can succeed to the goods of parents but not to their dignity, so also must succession to the throne of France pass according to the dictates of custom and divine will, and not individual desires. There are political dangers inherent in female rulers: the sense of continuity offered by patrilinear descent is lost, and queens may marry against the interests of their subjects. The fact that these arguments come after the case against Salic Law indicates that they are thought to be the more convincing (see above, 5.1.4).[27]

5.3.4   Renaissance jurists also consider the succession of women to fiefs. There are such things as 'feuda mulierum'; some abbesses can hold fiefs. But in general ('regulariter') women are excluded from succession to them. In the Middle Ages, Baldus had given five reasons for this: women cannot bear arms, they cannot mix freely with men without endangering their modesty, they have wayward judgement ('fragilitas consilii'), they are deceitful and do not keep their word, and finally they cannot keep secrets.[28] Girolamo Garzoni considers these reasons in his *Tractatus de feminis ad feuda recipiendis vel non* of 1580, and refutes them all, pointing to similar failings in men and examples of bellicose females and women with solid political judgement. He asserts that the exclusion of women from fiefs was a matter of custom, which men justified after the fact by the reasons given above.[29]

5.3.5   Garzoni shows some sympathy to woman, although he does not propose any change in the law; there are also Renaissance tracts which support the medieval view and uphold its reasoning. One such text is the *Certamen masculo-foemineum super aequitate utilitate et necessitate differentiarum sexus in successionibus, quibus extantibus masculis excluduntur foeminae: in Italia, Gallia, Hispania et Germania* ('A war of the sexes on the topic of the equity, utility and necessity of sex difference in succession, by which, in Italy, France, Spain and Germany, women are excluded if there are surviving males') which appears in Speyer in 1602 under the name of Gregorius Rolbag (although in 1606 it makes a second appearance with Jacobus Orloshaufen cited as its author[30]). This work is a dialectical presentation of the issue of female succession. It is divided into two 'battle lines', the *Acies muliebris* (whose arguments are rehearsed first) and the *Acies virilis* (which, coming second, is presumably meant to be interpreted as the victor). There are few

arguments which can be described as legal; most of the text is taken up
with commonplace assertions drawn from theology, medicine, ethics
and historical examples which set out to prove the superiority or
inferiority of women to men. A more precise legal debate arises over the
von Rechenberger/Sprintzenstein case (1614–15) in which the law
schools (*academiae*) of Ingolstadt and Rostock, respectively, are en-
gaged, suggesting that there may be a sectarian dimension to this
debate as well as the legal issue of inheritance. The literature suscitated by
the case is quite voluminous.[31] A less wide-ranging exchange of views
on the issue of female succession takes place in the mid seventeenth
century between Paganinus Gaudentius and I. N. Herzholmius, which,
like the *Certamen masculo-foemineum*, concerns itself with the natural
justification for exclusion.[32]

5.3.6   It has been said that abbesses can hold fiefs; this is the limit of
their powers, which are temporal and not spiritual. It seems, however,
that just as Garzoni wishes to obtain for woman more dignity in law, if
not a more equitable dispensation, so also do some canon lawyers wish to
enhance the standing of abbesses, although there is on this subject very
little room for manoeuvre. Etienne d'Alvin's treatise on the powers of
clergy of 1607 presents a more liberal view of the powers of abbesses by
procuration than that shown by Francisco de Vitoria (1480–1546?) in his
authoritative *Relectiones*, published in 1565.[33] We may again note a shift
in attitude towards the end of the sixteenth century (see above, 5.3.4),
accompanied by little real improvement in status. Such improvements
as occur in law are not discussed at all; they seem in general to concern
the rights and powers of widows, and commercial activities which allow
those who pursue them, without regard to sex, complete and free
enjoyment of the goods they administer or gain.

5.4.1   We may now turn to the relationship between sex difference
and other differences recognized in law. Marriage is perhaps the most
important of these. It is part of natural law (*Institutes*, 1.2.1), and is
inseparable from the notion of woman: 'all women are understood
either married, or to be married', as an English legal writer declares.[34]
Renaissance jurists often treat this subject eclectically, suggesting links
with theology, medicine, and ethics as well as rhetoric in the form of
treatises on the advisability of the married state. André Tiraqueau,
whose grasp of commonplaces about women drawn from the whole
range of scholarship is unrivalled, and Giovanni Nevizzano are
outstanding examples of this approach. The latter's *Sylva nuptialis* (1521)
is itself rhetorical in disposition, answering in turn the questions 'an sit

nubendum', and 'an non sit nubendum'; the former's treatise is an extended commentary on a section of the customary law of Poitou:

If man and woman, whether of noble birth or not, are married in Poitou according to its customary law, the woman is in the power of her husband, and is no longer in the power of her father, if she had one, and cannot make valid contracts without the express consent of her husband during their marriage, nor administer their common goods, nor her own, without the authority and consent of the said husband.[35]

5.4.2   According to these jurists, matrimony is a state which is more advantageous to women than to men (its etymology from *mater* is said to indicate this), and they are more concerned to convince men than women of its worth. The conditions for a good marriage depend not on the qualities of the husband (who is assumed to be a sound proposition, provided that he is endowed with good eyesight and is not too old), but on those of the wife, and the *caveats* about her suggest (facetiously) that a negative answer to the question 'an sit nubendum' is the safest. Annulment, divorce and polygamy are not of direct relevance to this study; it may simply be noted that Catholic jurists reproduce the strictures of Canon Law on annulment and divorce, and their protestant counterparts show great reluctance to consider them as anything other than extreme remedies for marital problems. Polygamy and con- cubinage, if discussed at all, are dismissed as contrary to natural law and divine commandment.[36] The place of woman in marriage is that prescribed by the Bible and moralistic literature; she should stay in the home and occupy herself there with suitable pursuits. She is the 'head and end of her family' ('caput et finis suae familiae': *Digest*, 50.16.195), who has a dowry in lieu of rights of succession. She is in all things subject to the authority of her husband and (except in cases of mental cruelty or impotence of the husband) cannot go to law without his consent. As well as authority over her goods, the husband has authority over her person, and may 'correct' or beat her to a 'reasonable degree'.[37] In English law, the married woman is treated as a wife, not as an *individuum*, since she is 'of one flesh' with her husband (Gen. 2: 24).[38] Her dignity is also that of her spouse.[39] For all this, she is a free person as a wife and not a servant.

5.4.3   Of the relationship of sex difference to social rank little need be said. A woman's place in the hierarchy of society is determined by her father or husband, and attracts the rights and duties of the rank in question. It has already been seen that different behaviour is expected from women of different social rank. The question of age and sex is of greater interest. In the *Lawes resolutions of women's rights* (pp. 7–8) there are said to be six ages between seven and twenty-one years at which different legal entitlements may be enjoyed. More generally, all law recognizes *puer* (*puella*), *virgo viripotens, marita, mater, gravida, lactans, vidua* as states in the life of woman which require special dispensation in law. These states are made up of the marriage paradigm (maiden/wife/ widow) and the physiological paradigm (*virgo/mulier/mater* etc.) which may not be those of the greatest anthropological or demographic interest, but underline the close bonds which link law to the disciplines of ethics and medicine.

5.4.4   There is a clear relationship between legal functions and sex difference. Woman is excluded from a wide variety of legal functions, including acting as witness, making contracts and administering property. These exclusions derive from two closely related forces in law: the first, the assumption that woman is mentally and physically weaker than man has been examined above (5.3.4); the second, consisting of the influence of *mores* and *consuetudo* (the established institutions and customs of society), is reflected both in the respect shown for marriage (see above, 5.4.1–5.4.2) and in the belief that law should uphold tradition as this mirrors natural hierarchies (cf. *Institutes*, 1.3.9). When the question of office or profession is raised in relation to women, the same arguments from nature, custom and institutions are rehearsed. A frequently quoted commonplace on this topic is taken from *Digest*, 50.17.2 (*De regulis juris antiqui*):

Women are excluded from all civil and public offices; and thus they may not be *judices*, nor magistrates, nor advocates; nor may they intervene on another's behalf in law, nor act as agents.[40]

The *De regulis juris antiqui* attracts a certain number of commentaries between 1499 and 1576 which are published together in a collected edition in 1593. The five commentators (Philippus Francus (de Franchi) (fl. 1499), Philippus Decius (de Dexia) (1454–1535), Johannes Ferrarius (d. 1558), Girolamo Cagnoli (1493?–1551), Jakob Raevardus (1536–68))[41] all write on this *regula*, providing definitions of woman, justifications of her inferior status drawn from many sources, and examples of her prerogatives in law as well as her disadvantages, which were first assembled by Joannes Bassianus as early as the twelfth century.[42]

5.4.5   Although citing examples of women holding public office in different societies (Sparta, ancient Gaul, the Celtic tribes and ancient Germany),[43] nearly all commentators approve of this exclusion, and adduce reasons not only from parallel sources such as the Bible and ethical texts, but also from legal writings. As above, the reasons for exclusion relate either to the established institutions of society, which require that woman act with greater modesty than man, as she is the guardian of chastity, which in turn is the guarantee of patrilinearity (*Digest*, 23.2.43 (gloss), 'in muliere maior honestas requiritur'); or the natural frailty of woman; or finally *consuetudo*, which here is said to derive from a historical event (Calpurnia's notorious behaviour).[44] Examples from contemporary or near-contemporary history are sometimes adduced in support of these arguments.[45] Of the reasons given, it is usual to give priority to *mores* and *consuetudo*,[46] suggesting a similar conservatism to that which was encountered in ethics (see above, 4.4.5).

5.5.1   This exclusion leads naturally to a discussion of the *deterior conditio* of woman in law (*Digest*, 1.9.5). Woman's debarment from succession, office and privilege is justified by her *levitas, fragilitas, imbecillitas, infirmitas*. These words recur often in the *Digest*, and in legal texts of the Renaissance;[47] they are often linked with a recital of female vices, grouped according to their relationship to avarice, ambition and sensuality (see above, 2.11.2).[48] By custom, as well as by nature, 'greater dignity resides in the male sex' ('maior dignitas est in sexu virili', *Digest*, 1.9.1), and men should be preferred, other things being equal, to women in all offices to which both are eligible. The physical infirmity of women leads lawyers to presume that of twins of both sexes, the male is the first born (*Digest*, 34.5.10), and that on occasions on which both man and wife die at more or less the same time, it is to be presumed that the woman, being weaker, died first (*Digest*, 34.5.8, 25.1.32). A woman is also to be tortured before a man whenever both sexes are put to the question, because 'she has a weak and unstable constitution' ('momentaneum et instabile cor habet', *Digest*, 48.18.18 (gloss)), and will confess the sooner.[49] In adultery, the crime of woman is greater, for she has visibly committed an improper act if pregnancy ensues (see above, 2.7.1). In general, nature enjoins on woman the (quasi-)virtue of *verecundia* or shame, which should keep her out of the public eye (see above, 4.5.3). In cases where she is allowed to testify, she is thought to be less credible than male witnesses (*Digest*, 22.4.6).

5.5.2   In some areas of law woman is the equal of man. According to natural law, men and women 'are to be treated as equals';[50] this relates to their community of species and theoretical equality in the Bible. For this reason, both sexes are considered to merit equal punishment in criminal law, although pregnant women and mothers of newborn children have certain prerogatives, and there are others, as we shall see, which derive from assumptions of diminished responsibility. Women are also of course exempt from crimes of a sexual nature, such as rape and forced marriage, and from clauses relating to offices which they cannot fill; otherwise, as Godefroy and Goeddaeus point out, *masculus* in general implies also *femina*, and vice versa.

5.5.3   Women's prerogatives in law derive also from their allegedly weaker physical and mental powers, and from *mores* and *consuetudo*. Women are in general not incarcerated, nor can they be compelled to appear before a court. They are excused ignorance of the law (although not, it seems, in England[51]): they are assumed, with rustics and the simple-minded, to act often against their own best interest because of weakheadedness ('mulier adversus contra propria commoda laborat', *Codex*, 5.4.4). They are excused, because of their timid nature, actions committed while in the grip of fear more readily than is man ('mulier pro minori metu excusatur quam masculus'). They are assumed to be simple-minded ('in muliere et rustico praesumitur simplicitas', *Codex*, 4.64 [*nota Baldi*]). They come of age earlier than men for legal purposes. They are excused hanging and torture if pregnant. The advantages deriving from custom include the impossibility of their committing the crime of *lèse-majesté*.[52] There is little which enhances the dignity of woman in these prerogatives: nearly all derive from assumptions of physical or mental weakness, supposed irresponsibility and *de facto* exclusion from public office.

5.6.1   For all this, it seems clear, as in the case of medicine (see above, 3.9.2), that lawyers in the early seventeenth century believe themselves to present a point of view or an interpretation of law more in favour of woman than their scholastic counterparts. This is not an easy task, as Roman Law proper, with the exception of the repeal of the *lex Voconia*, tends to degrade, not improve the position of women.[53] Examples of feminist lawyers are Johannes Ulricus Wolff (*Discursus: de foeminarum in jure civili et canonico privilegiis, immunitatibus et praeeminentia*, 1615) and the satirist Joachimus Eberartus (*Bonus* [*sic*] *mulier*, 1616). Both write vehemently against 'anti-feminist' jurists such as Jacques Cujas, both denounce the *Disputatio nova contra mulieres*; Wolff goes so far as to address woman in general and exhorts her to admire the efforts he has made on her behalf. He also lists 'good' lawyers and 'bad' lawyers with

regard to the problem of woman, although in retrospect the difference
between the two may not seem to be great.[54] The running head of *The
Lawes resolutions of women's rights* – 'The woman's lawier' – even suggests
that it is a manual intended for the use of women; and it has been argued
that, in England at least, there is some evidence of a real improvement in
the legal dispensation for women between 1400 and 1600, of which this
running head might be an expression.[55]

5.6.2   Such legal feminism had already found expression in feminist
tracts, such as Henricus Cornelius Agrippa's seminal *De nobilitate et
praecellentia foeminei sexus . . . declamatio* (1529):

> By the excessive power of male tyranny, which prevails against divine justice
> and the laws of nature, women's liberty is denied to them by law, suppressed by
> custom and usage, and eradicated by upbringing. For as soon as a woman is
> born, she is imprisoned in the home in a state of idleness from her earliest years
> on, and is not allowed to wield anything other than needle and thread, as
> though she were incapable of more lofty activities. Once she has reached the age
> of puberty, she is given over into the jealous control of a husband, or shut up for
> ever in the vestals' prison . . . she is excluded from public and civil offices by
> law: furthermore she is debarred from jurisdiction, judgement, adoption, from
> giving surety, from acting on another's behalf, from tutelage, from
> guardianship, from criminal cases and cases concerning wills . . .[56]

This may appear to be a clarion call to radical change; but it would be
safer to regard it as part of a rhetorical exercise in declamation. A similar
reference to the denial of woman's rights is found in *The Lawes
resolutions of women's rights*, but attributed to Eve's malediction, and
passed over without further comment.[57]

5.6.3   If there is a feminist movement in law, its room for manoeuvre
is very restricted. The institution of marriage profoundly affects
woman's status; authority, responsibility, property and dignity are
vested in the husband. Her supposed physical and mental weaknesses
deprive her of public functions, if they confer certain dubious privileges.
Her equality under natural law is recognized neither in the social
dispensation of Roman times nor in that of the Renaissance, and *mores* as
well as *consuetudo* are powerful forces in legal thought. Sympathy with
her plight, belief in her dignity may not be uncommon, but it is difficult
to see how such sentiments could attain practical expression in the real
world. It seems that this is only possible in the one area in which woman
is not firmly attached to the notion of marriage, namely widowhood;
and in law relating to developing economic activities such as commerce.
A feminist lawyer in the Renaissance is one who pleads for the

recognition of the dignity of woman; he may, in doing this, refer to the developments in other disciplines (such as the rejection of the medical argument of female imperfection) in order to reinforce his plea. His task is to some extent made easier at the end of the Renaissance by the expurgation of medieval glosses from the Corpus Juris Civilis, which leads to the suppression in the text of many anti-feminist comments and elucidations.

5.6.4   But as well as established institutions such as marriage, the nature of sex difference in law prevents sweeping advances. Difference in law consists of contraries (married/unmarried) or opposites of privation (able to succeed to a title/unable to succeed). There is little room for the 'species relativa' which has its place in medicine and ethics. Furthermore, in law a person is often considered to be inseparable from function, title, property or deed; woman is unable to fulfil most functions, she is given title and property only by virtue of husband or father, and is possessed solely of the dubious privilege of equality with man as a criminal. In spite of regional and national differences, the principle of woman's inferiority is almost universal. It is to be found in the substratum of legal thought, in which there are strong links forged with theology, medicine and ethics. It is not important for the purposes of this study to know whether these links constitute *a posteriori* justifications of the status quo, or provide *a priori* principles on which to build laws; it seems that both possibilities are accepted by Renaissance jurists. Those who continue to make links with other disciplines after the development of the 'mos gallicus' may be less numerous by 1600; but even scholars who relate woman's status to historical moment and to cultural attitudes (such as Baudouin and Garzoni) make little impact in their own time. The historicism which transforms the study of all branches of law in the sixteenth century has little direct bearing on the notional legal status of the female sex.

6

Conclusion

6.1.1   Why do certain aspects of the notion of woman not change, while others undergo modification during the Renaissance? What are the main differences in the notion of woman which take place during this period? Is there a Renaissance 'feminist' movement (that is, a movement to improve the notional status of woman *vis-à-vis* man), and in what does it consist? The answers offered to these questions are necessarily tentative, as they relate to a study of fragmentary evidence culled from texts widely separated in date and place of publication. They are also offered in the awareness that the notion of woman has a wider context than that which has been considered here, and that it is affected by changes to the notion of 'human being' and 'male' which merit further investigation.

6.1.2   The main causes for stasis in the notion of woman which emerge from this study are, in different contexts, the desire to foster and preserve the scholastic synthesis, and the influence on thought of the institution of matrimony. The first of these causes is apparent in the interdisciplinary and recuperative features of theological, medical, moral and legal texts, and in the transmission of information between disciplines in the form of commonplaces. For a synthesis to be effective, it must embrace the whole encyclopaedia of knowledge, and must account for all known evidence, using a method adaptable to each individual discipline. The recuperation of all evidence into a single scheme is evident in theology in the four senses of Scripture (see above, 2.1.3); in medicine in the adage 'nature makes nothing in vain' (Aristotle, *De partibus animalium*, III.1 [661*b* 25], IV.11 [691*b* 5], Galen, *De usu partium corporis*, X.14); in law in the desire to legislate for all persons, things and actions (see above, 5.1.4). In ethics and politics, the principle of recuperation is embodied in the method of analysis, which shares its terminology with other Aristotelian disciplines. An effect of recuperation is the unwillingness on the part of the interpreter to accept as coherent that which has not been, or cannot easily be, resolved into the general pattern. This is well expressed in Blaise Pascal's *Pensées*: 'every author has a meaning with which all of the contradictory parts of his work are consistent, or else he has no meaning at all'.[1]

6.1.3   Interdisciplinarity does not necessarily imply that all related disciplines are of the same order, or bear the same authority. In one sense at least, theology in Christian Europe precedes ethics, law and medicine. In another sense, the organon in which Aristotelian method is established precedes these disciplines. Medicine can be said to precede ethics, as it provides natural justifications for moral and political precepts; both medicine and ethics underlie law. The relationship between disciplines is not, however, uniquely hierarchical; it is also molecular, for different disciplines reflect different aspects of human existence. Any movement of ideas between disciplines represents therefore a complex translation, involving both change of procedures and language. The associations – literal and metaphorical – of the words *mulier*, *femina*, *muliebris*, *effeminatus* have been seen to be different according to discipline. They are, however, not so widely divergent as to deter Renaissance scholars from pluridisciplinary approaches as well as from simple reference to the conclusions of other disciplines. André Tiraqueau's account of woman in his *De legibus connubialibus* of 1513 is pluridisciplinary: later examples of the same approach can be found in the work of Francisco de Valles (1588) and Simon Majolus (1597).[2] One important reason why these and other scholars are able to write eclectically about woman in spite of the difficulties involved is the remarkable concordance of views in Judaeo-Christian and classical writings about her inferiority to the male. The manner of Eve's creation suggests the lower status embodied in the *mas occasionatus* theory; the first sin recalls the jurist's belief in woman's *imbecillitas animi*; the curse of subordination to husband equates with woman's *deterior conditio* in law; the 'Alphabet of the Good Woman' in Proverbs is consistent with Aristotle's division between conservative and acquisitive rôles in the household for woman and man. The comprehensive nature of this concordance disguises the differences between Judaeo-Christian and pagan thought.

6.1.4   The borrowing of supporting material from other disciplines may thus be said to contribute to the continuing belief in female inferiority.[3] There are also conservative forces at work within disciplines. The traditional methods of interpretation in theology are preserved by neoscholastic writers – both Catholic and protestant – in spite of the emergence of biblical scholarship and the work of evangelical humanists. In medicine, although Galen supplants Avicenna to a large degree as the leading authority, and although new experimental medicine begins to make significant advances, the *problématique* – the questions asked of the evidence – has still to evolve. In ethics and politics change does occur where a writer is not interpreting a given text; but in commentaries on the *Nicomachean Ethics* and the *Politics*, there are scant indications of a historicist approach which would allow for a reinterpretation of the place of woman. In law, although this historicist approach is developed, certain institutions, notably marriage, hinder development in areas concerning the notion under scrutiny here.

6.1.5   Interdisciplinarity is effected often by the transmission of information in the form of commonplaces. These belong, in rhetorical terms, to the sphere of *inventio*, or the assembling of relevant material for an argument or demonstration. They act as assertions which are authoritative in a given context. There are many commonplace books produced in the Renaissance, sometimes in the form of collections of related adages for the use of preachers or poets, sometimes in essay form, as is the case in the works of Alessandro d'Alessandro (*c.* 1463–1521), Pietro Crinito (1465–1505), Jean Tixier de Ravisi (Ravisius Textor) (d. 1524?), and Lodovico Ricchieri (Caelius Rhodiginus) (1453?–1525?).[4] Perhaps the most ambitious of these compendia is that of Giovanni Battista Bernardo of Venice, entitled *Seminarium totius philosophiae Aristotelicae, Platonicae et Stoicae* (1597–1605), which presents commonplaces alphabetically by subject. When they treat of woman, the majority of these books reproduce arguments relating to her inferiority; even where sections are devoted to heroic or otherwise notable women, the wider context suggests that such examples are exceptions to the rule.

6.1.6   In a different way, the influence on thought of the institution of marriage may be said to prevent fundamental changes in the notion of woman during the Renaissance. Matrimony is a divine, natural and social institution in the eyes of Renaissance thinkers: any alternative is theologically contentious, and requires a new vision of the mental and physical predispositions of the sexes. Even in such imaginary societies as St Thomas More's Utopia and François Rabelais's Abbaye de Thélème it continues to play a part.[5] By the late Renaissance, there is still no change in its divine authority for Catholic and reformed thinkers alike; its natural justification on physiological grounds has not been seriously impugned; only the psychological justification of the subjection of woman has come under consistent attack in works where she is accorded parity with man in the 'operationes animi'. Even if the injustice of certain aspects of the institution is recognized, the status quo is still generally defended in the name of religious orthodoxy or a conservatism based on the belief that change in itself is bad. Marriage is an immovable obstacle to any improvement in the theoretical or real status of woman in law, in theology, in moral and political philosophy. Its influence is even apparent in medicine, whence comes its 'natural' justification.

6.2.1   The forces which foster change are found both within and outside intellectual life: humanism in its various manifestations, and contemporary events and thought in the spheres of religion, society, politics and economics. The revision and rediscovery of ancient literature cannot be said to be a great factor in changes in the notion of woman; only in medicine are significant new texts widely disseminated, and as has been seen, these do not speak unequivocally in favour of woman. More important are the new philosophies which emerge in the Renaissance. Neoplatonism is influential in the promotion of new ideas on woman in two domains: the theory of love and politics. There can be no doubt that the respect and honour paid to the female sex in the love poetry and the pastoral of Renaissance Europe is closely connected with the neoplatonist theory of beauty and love. The passage of the *Republic* in which Socrates argues that women should be allowed to participate in the running of the state is widely known and quoted, and opposed to the Aristotelian view. Neostoicism enhances the dignity of the individual by presenting him or her with the possibility of achieving apathy and practising the virtue of *constantia*, in spite of personal or political vicissitudes; although not explicitly applied to women by theorists such as Justus Lipsius and Guillaume Du Vair, it is adapted for their purposes by seventeenth-century moralists. It has been seen, however, that neoplatonism and neostoicism, albeit widely celebrated and influential, do not altogether liberate Renaissance thought about woman from its scholastic axes. This is more effectively done by thinkers such as Paracelsus or Postel, who attempt to discard not only scholastic method but also its language; and by those who employ intellectual satire to this end.

6.2.2   We have encountered one Renaissance intellectual joke – 'woman is not a human being' – in three contexts: theology, medicine and law (see above, 2.4.2, 3.2.2, 5.2.1). In each case, it seems that the satire is directed against an object other than woman: socinianism, prejudice, academic ponderousness. In each case, the effect of the joke is to reinforce the contrary proposition: woman is a human being. It may be coincidental that woman is chosen as a vehicle for satire in this way; or it may be that she is particularly well suited to be such a vehicle, as it will be evident to those to whom the satire is addressed that there is a discrepancy between what she is and what she is said to be according to traditional authorities. One way of escaping from the infrastructure of scholastic thought would thus appear to be by the use of humour. This would explain why contemporary thinkers take texts seriously which are clearly signposted as flippant, or which actually advertise their flippancy: the *Disputatio nova contra mulieres*, Erasmus's *Praise of Folly*, Scaliger's *Exercitationes*.

6.2.3   An area of humanistic thought which promises to open the way for a new interpretation of woman is historicism. If this were to be applied to an ancient or even theological text, it would reveal the relativity between statements about woman and the cultural identity of their author. Thus, on the one hand, Aristotle's slighting comments about woman in politics could be related to his expectations and presuppositions as a fourth-century Athenian; on the other, examples of outstanding women and gynaecocratic cultures of the past (e.g. the Amazons) cease to be departures from the norm but might be explained by the relationship between the culture in question and its attitudes to the female sex. This process is begun in the Renaissance in certain texts dealing with government by women such as Elizabeth I and Catherine de Médicis. It is impeded by the sectarian and national dimensions to the debate about Salic Law, which encourage many writers to appeal to authoritative statements about woman's incapacity to rule; it is also inhibited by the Christian institution of marriage, which cannot lightly be dismissed as part of European culture, and which restricts any fundamental reassessment of woman and her rôle in society.

6.2.4   In the domain of medicine, scientific experiment and observation are forces for change which affect the notion of woman. They concur well with functionalism as a heuristic procedure, present in Aristotle and Galen in different measures, but developed by Renaissance anatomists and physiologists, and responsible for the major changes in the notion of woman in the course of the sixteenth century. The rejection of the parallels male/female, active/passive, formal/material, perfect/deprived does not, however, occur in all contexts where sex difference is in question. Even after the refutation of the arguments of *mas occasionatus* and ineffective semen, 'female' can still imply deprivation. The clearest examples of this are found in discussions of the psychology of woman, which extend into ethics and politics as well as medicine. The idea of sex difference in these disciplines incorporates the opposite of privation (see above, 4.3.2), that of relation (see above, 4.5.2) and can generate contradiction (see above, 4.6.5). In common also with medical studies, ethics and politics reflect the renewed interest in functionalism, especially in the work of Montecatini. But the relationship of ethics to empirical data is rather different from that which was seen to be the case in medicine. The objective status of observation is not so well established, and theories cannot be tested in the same way. Psychological models, whether Aristotelian or neostoic, are, in one sense at least, linguistic strategies or arbitrary conceptual structures by which to classify and explain diverse human actions. In the case of scholastic faculty psychology, notions of 'will', 'reason', 'passion' are not thought by the end of the Renaissance to convey objective facts about the human mind and its physiological affinities, but are seen as words which designate in an organized fashion interrelationships which can only be analysed – and perhaps which only exist – in discourse. Such an attitude is embodied in Montaigne's comment on the scholastic definition of man as 'animal rationale ac mortale': 'I know better what a man is, than I know what is "animal" or "mortal" or "rational"'.[6] For doctors and lawyers, and to some degree for political philosophers also, words are signs which represent verifiable facts about human beings and human actions: 'words signify, things are signified', says the gloss on *Digest*, 50.16.1.[7] For moralists on the other hand, language is more a web which offers no escape, not a transparent window on to an object or action.

6.2.5   It has been seen that much discussion about woman is governed or underlaid by a theory of opposites and of difference. Similarity and difference are of course fundamental to any perception of reality or discourse about it; we are all alike as human beings, and distinct from other species, and as individuals we are all distinct from each other.[8] The willingness to see objects as similar, and the desire to distinguish objects as finely as possible, have been shown to be related to radical or conservative patterns of thought;[9] Renaissance theology and law reflect in the main a conservative view of sex, linking it to the opposite of privation and to contrariety. In ethics and medicine, the 'species relativa' is more in evidence, and one may detect a continuum of change rather than discontinuity (see above, 3.9.5, 4.2.2). But even in these disciplines, the conservative view of sex difference survives, and causes notable dislocations of thought, especially where psychology is in question. Underlying this Aristotelian taxonomy of opposition are Pythagorean dualities, which link, without explanation, woman with imperfection, left, dark, evil and so on. These emerge most obviously in medicine, but are implied in theology and ethics also. Although they are nowhere explicitly defended, they may nonetheless be the most accurate indicator in anthropological terms of the status of woman in Renaissance society and culture. The connection of woman with imperfection and evil may well have deeper mystical than scholastic roots.

6.3.1   Social, religious, political, economic factors influence intellectual debate in still less commensurable ways. This topic is particularly difficult in relation to woman, as the most interesting demographic and anthropological categories of womanhood do not coincide with those which are discussed by scholars in the Renaissance.[10] One may with great caution suggest two forces for change in society: the modification in social class divisions which brings greater mobility between classes and promotes the emergence of a social group of rich, leisured women below the level of court and salon, but above that of peasantry and artisans;[11] the second force, related to the first, is reflected in the courtesy books of the Renaissance, suggesting the development of social life in this new class and its theory and expectations of social behaviour.[12] In the domain of religion, one might point to the effects of Bible reading and literacy on protestant women and the protestant family,[13] and, in a Catholic context, charitable and mystical activities by women which reflect the use of religion as an outlet for female social and intellectual energies which were stifled in secular society. The examples of queen regents and female monarchs are clearly influential on intellectual debate in the political sphere; in that of economic life, the success of widows as administrators of their husbands' estates and businesses, and that of women in commercial activities which were open to them may be singled out as significant forces for a change in attitudes.

6.3.2   It seems appropriate at this point to mention a curious omission from Renaissance discussions of woman. Except in technical treatises on witchcraft, it is rare to find mention of sorcery in connection with woman, although, as has been shown, it is a significant feature of the anthropology of late Renaissance Europe.[14] This absence of discussion may in part be due to the fact that sorcery applies to both sexes, although its manifestation is more dramatic in woman because she is 'possessed' (just as, in the terms of human relationships, she is given a passive and self-abnegatory rôle) and therefore more deeply tinged with evil.[15] The prosecution of widowed or single women as witches may be due also to an unspoken fear of abandoning the traditional view of woman as a person married or destined for marriage; this is consistent with suggestions already made about the institution of matrimony as a conservative influence on thought. It may therefore add anthropological evidence to that which has been brought forward in this study from the realm of intellectual history.

6.3.3   It is tempting, in spite of regional differences, to try to put approximate dates to changes in the notion of woman in the republic of letters. Wide divergences appear if individual disciplines are examined; the publication of new texts, the results of experiment, and historical events such as the Council of Trent and the accession of female rulers are examples of influential factors. In spite of these divergences, it may be suggested that the half century between 1580 and 1630 sees most single-discipline and interdisciplinary activity. This may in part be due to the vigorous scholarly climate; it is also linked with the satirical debates about woman (see above, 6.2.2). Between these dates, the list of works which propose, in a serious scholarly context, some revision in the notion and status of woman is impressive, as has been seen; they precede and accompany a rash of feminist polemic throughout Europe (see below, 6.5.2). From this one may tentatively conclude that the latter part of the sixteenth century and the early part of the seventeenth witnessed a shift in scholarly attitudes to the female sex which is reflected in more popular polemical works. This is not to say that previous intellectual debates (reflected in earlier popular feminist polemic) had not wrought changes in scholarly attitudes to woman; but that the synthetic, scholastic view is attacked for the first time as a whole.

6.4.1   The interdisciplinary notion of woman represented in such writings as Tiraqueau's *De legibus connubialibus* is clearly no longer tenable in 1630, but some parts of it survive, producing dislocations of thought especially in the area of psychology. Cold and moist humours are associated with lack of judgement, of courage and of stamina, instability, untrustworthiness, and passivity. Such mental features can be described as effeminate, since cold and moist humours are dominant in woman; their contraries can be described as virile. Certain Renaissance scholars suggest that this association of humours and mental operations is false or misleading; others, turning to neostoic psychology, stress the rôle of will and reason in the control of bodily passions, and thus dissociate humours from mental behaviour, even if retaining a link between the body and the passions. In both cases, inconsistency is encountered when these arguments are aligned with other aspects of medical science (such as the effect of the uterus on the mind), or with other disciplines in which woman's mental inferiority is still accepted (theology, ethics, politics, law). When theologians, moralists and jurists declare that women are equal in the operations of the mind, they must do so either by postulating a historical dimension to authoritative texts, so that the limitations of past knowledge do not inhibit the proper interpretation of the modern world; or by having recourse to linguistic strategies (metaphorical, allegorical, anagogical senses). In the first case, it is necessary as a first step to recognize that ideas and institutions are relative to the cultures in which they are found. This in turn would lead to the discussion of possible modifications in the institutions of a culture if the ideas which justified them are rejected. Such a step is not taken with regard to woman, whose fate is closely linked to the impregnable institution of marriage, as has already been noted.

6.4.2   Linguistic strategies can resolve contradictions and dislocations in thought; they can also act on it as conservative forces. Metaphorical understandings of 'woman' are found in both theology and medicine; they are closely related to notions of passivity, receptivity, mutability, sensuality, frailty and deprivation. Such ideas help to maintain scholastic attitudes to the female sex. Neoplatonist writers on the other hand stress the spirituality of woman and her close link with mysteries; these new metaphorical associations are reinforced by elements of the Christian tradition, notably Marianism, which flourished with particular force throughout Catholic Europe after the Council of Trent.[16] The emblematic representations of pagan goddesses, and the Renaissance portrayal of virtues as female figures (female because of the Latin gender) also add to the metaphorical dignity of woman, as baroque artists themselves point out. It is in this sphere of female representation in the visual arts that the most evident advances are made over the medieval period; they reflect a new appreciation of female beauty which may be linked also with the banishment of notions of uncleanness (see above, 3.6.1). The portrayal of active, heroic females also contrasts with the passive iconographical portrayal of woman, who as a symbolic embodiment mirrors the virtue or vice in question rather than exemplifying it in an active way.[17]

6.5.1   I have noted the presence in the disciplines of medicine and law of scholars who believe that they are writing in a feminist way; that is, proposing a reassessment of woman *vis-à-vis* man in favour of the former. There is also a considerable body of writing which is uniquely feminist in its aims, setting out to prove either that woman is superior to man or (more rarely) that she is his equal. This has its origins in the Middle Ages, and in many cases is governed in its expression by rhetoric.

The argument that woman is superior to man is paradoxical in the Renaissance except in certain neoplatonist contexts, and demands a certain sort of demonstration, exemplified by Cornelius Agrippa's *De nobilitate et praecellentia foeminei sexus...declamatio* (1529), and later codified by Nicodemus Frischlin (1547–90) in a work entitled *Methodus declamandi in laudatione, thesi de laudibus mulierum demonstrata* (1606). Among the arguments rehearsed by many feminist writers is the series of theological proofs of female excellence *e nomine* (in Hebrew, Eve means life, Adam means earth), *ex ordine* (Eve was the last created thing, and therefore God's masterpiece), *e materia* (Eve was made of living flesh, whereas Adam was made of earth), *e loco* (Eve was created in paradise, Adam outside) and *e conceptione* (woman bore God, which man could not do). These 'proofs' are clearly inconsistent with the wider context of theology; Agrippa himself admits that, in declamations of the sort he wrote in favour of woman, there are many invalid arguments and jests.[18] For all this, as with intellectual satire (see above, 6.2.2), it would be unwise to assume that there is nothing but flippancy in the writer's purpose, even if the genre as a whole was intended to amuse rather than persuade. As in the case of intellectual jokes, the humour may indicate the impossibility of discussing in serious terms the proposition of woman's equality, and therefore represents a strategy of discourse which is subversive in intention.[19] It should also be pointed out that the question of equality is not simple; various models of equalization of the sexes are considered, which reflect differing priorities and differing degrees of conservatism (cf. above, 4.4.5–4.4.7).[20]

6.5.2   An indication of the link between feminist writing and intellectual debate about woman is found in the polemics which occur throughout Europe at the end of the sixteenth century and the beginning of the seventeenth. In France, in England, in Italy, in Germany, in Holland, anti-feminist texts (including the pseudo-anti-feminist *Disputatio nova contra mulieres*) provoke vigorous replies which often reflect the new aspects of the notion of woman discussed above. The writers of these replies are not only men; women also defend their own cause.[21] In many of their works may be detected an awareness of their subjection which previously had not received anything more than sporadic literary expression. Yet for all the advances made in Renaissance thought on this topic, the proposition that woman is equal or superior to man can still be held to be a paradox, and exploited for its artistic potential, in the middle years of the seventeenth century. This may be interpreted, however, as a late flowering of the awareness of dislocations in the notion of woman which heralds the end of a synthetic view founded in scholasticism.

6.5.3   In his *Dialogo sopra i due massimi sistemi del mondo* (1632), Galileo describes the decline of Aristotelianism in an elegant architectural metaphor. The enlightened modern philosopher Sagredo is commiserating with the staunch peripatetic Simplicio:

> I can put myself in Simplicio's place and see that he is deeply moved by the overwhelming force of these conclusive arguments. But seeing on the other hand the great authority that Aristotle has gained universally; considering the number of famous interpreters who have toiled to explain his meanings; and observing that the other sciences, so useful and necessary to mankind, base a large part of their value and reputation upon Aristotle's credit; Simplicio is confused and perplexed, and I seem to hear him say, 'Who would there be to settle our controversies if Aristotle were to be deposed? What other author should we follow in the schools, the academies, the universities? What philosopher has written the whole of natural philosophy, so well arranged, without omitting a single conclusion? Ought we to desert that structure under which so many travelers have recuperated? Should we destroy that haven, that Prytaneum where so many scholars have taken refuge so comfortably; where, without exposing themselves to the inclemencies of the air, they can acquire a complete knowledge of the universe by merely turning over a few pages? Should that fort be leveled where one may abide in safety against all enemy assaults?
>
> I pity him no less than I should some fine gentleman who, having built a magnificent palace at great trouble and expense, employing hundreds and hundreds of artisans, and then beholding it threatened with ruin because of poor foundations, should attempt, in order to avoid the grief of seeing the walls destroyed, adorned as they are with so many lovely murals; or the columns fall, which sustain the superb galleries, or the gilded beams; or the doors spoiled, or the pediments and the marble cornices, brought in at so much cost – should attempt, I say, to prevent the collapse with chains, props, iron bars, buttresses, and shores.[22]

Part of the collapse predicted here will bring down the Aristotelian notion of woman; but as this is closely related to the foundations of the building, it survives longer than many elements built on the infrastructure of inherited medieval thought. Even in the 1713 edition of Bartolomeo Castelli's *Lexicon medicum graeco-latinum* 'imperfectior mare' is still given as one epithet of *femina*; in popular culture, the idea of female inferiority has a yet longer history. Humanism, which did much to enhance the dignity of man, was long in liberating the 'man foeminine' from her subordinate status.

Appendix

THEOLOGY
Chap. 2 n.11
Aquinas, *Summa*, 1a 92,1: 'videtur quod mulier non debuit produci in prima rerum productione. Dicit enim Philosophus quod *femina est mas occasionatus*. Sed nihil occasionatum et deficiens debuit esse in prima rerum institutione; ergo in illa prima rerum institutione mulier producenda non fuit...Per respectum ad naturam particuliarem femina est aliquid deficiens et occasionatum. Quia virtus activa quae est in semine maris intendit producere sibi simile, perfectum secundum masculinum sexum; sed quod femina generetur, hoc est propter virtutis activae debilitatem, vel propter aliquam materiae indispositionem, vel etiam propter aliquam transmutationem ab extrinseco, puta a ventis australibus, qui sunt humidi ut dicitur in libro *De generatione animalium* [IV.2 [766*b* 33]].

Sed per comparationem ad naturam universalem femina non est aliquid occasionatum, sed est de intentione naturae, ad opus generationis ordinata. Intentio autem naturae universalis dependet ex Deo, qui est universalis auctor naturae. Et ideo instituendo naturam non solum marem sed etiam feminam produxit.'

Chap. 2 n.12
Cajetan, *Commentarii in quinque Mosaicos libros*, Paris, 1539, p. 25: 'id quod philosophi tradiderunt de .productione mulieris quae est vir laesus, hoc Moses sub metaphora tradidit. Multum tamen interest inter considerationem philosophorum et Mosi: quoniam illi productionem mulieris relative ad sexum consideraverunt, Moses vero productionem mulieris non solum ad sexum sed ad universam vitam moralem tradidit. Et propterea metaphora usus est constante ex multis partibus...Et ut metaphorice somnus [Ade] intelligeretur, describitur Adam dormisse, et tamen non describitur ipsum experge factum fuisse seu evigilasse. Somnus enim profundus immissus Deo viro ex quo producenda est mulier, similitudinem gerit defectus virtutis virilis unde naturaliter producitur mulier. Homo enim dormiens semihomo est. Et similiter principium generans mulierem semivirile est. Et propterea a philosophis mulier dicitur mas laesus.'

Chap. 2 n.16
Luther, *Werke*, Weimar, 1883– , XLII.51–2: 'ne videretur mulier excludi ab omni gloria futurae vitae, comprehendit Moses utrunque sexum, videtur enim mulier quoddam diversum animal a viro, quod et membra habet dissimilia, et ingenium longe infirmius. Ac quamvis Heva fuerit praestantissima creatura, similis Adae, quod ad imaginem Dei attinet, hoc est, ad iusticiam, sapientiam et salutem, tamen fuit mulier. Sicut enim sol praestantior est luna (quanquam luna quoque sit praestantissimum corpus), Ita mulier, etsi esset pulcherrimum opus Dei, tamen non aequabat gloriam et dignitatem masculi.'

Chap 2 n.26
Cornelius a Lapide, *In omnes divi Pauli epistolas commentaria*, Paris, 1638, pp. 284–5: 'mulier, puta coniux est viri gloria, id est gloriosa imago, ut dixi supra: quia Deus mulierem, scilicet Evam, formavit ex viro, ad viri similitudinem, ut virum tanquam suum exemplar ipsa quasi imago repraesentaret. Si ita est haec imago in mente et ratione; quod scilicet mulier instar viri sit praedita anima rationali, intellectu, voluntate, memoria, libertate, capaxque sit omnis sapientiae, gratiae et gloriae aeque ac vir; ac proinde mulier est imago viri, non proprie; nam mulier in anima rationali par est et aequalis viro; et uterque, scilicet tam mulier quam vir, factus est ad imaginem Dei; sed improprie et analogice; quia scilicet mulier tanquam posterior et inferior facta est ex viro, illique similis creata est. Unde Apostolus non expresse dicit, Mulier est imago viri, sed tantum, *Mulier est gloria viri*: quia nimirum, ut recte annotavit Salmeron, mulier est insigne viri ornamentum, utpote quae viro data est, tum in adiutorium ad propagandam liberos, et ad familiam gubernandam, tum in materiam, et quasi ditionem, in quam vir exerceat suam iurisdictionem et dominium. Dominium enim viri non tantum se extendit ad inanima et animalia bruta, sed etiam ad rationalia, puta ad mulieres et coniuges.'

Chap. 2 n.70
Machon, *Discours ou sermon en faveur des femmes*, Paris, 1641, pp. 34–5: 'quand l'Autheur de l'Ecclesiastique a mis en avant cet enigme, ou plustost ce Paradoxe, il semble que par une addresse toute Divine et merveilleuse, il ait voulu apporter un contrepoid égal à l'orgueil et présomption des femmes, qui de leur naturel est[aient] toutes paistries dedans la vanité, et l'amour d'elles-mesmes; par une saincte apparence, et un remède plus salutaire qu'agréable, a feint de mespriser jusqu'à leur propre vertu, prévoyant bien qu'elles trouveroient assez de moyens et d'artifices, pour s'eslever plus qu'elles ne doivent, et s'en faire accroître beaucoup davantage qu'il n'en est pas.'

Chap. 2 n.103
Peter Martyr Vermigli, *Loci communes*, IV.1, pp. 588–9: 'neque arbitror esse negandum, aliquas ex mulieribus prophetiae dono instructas populum publice

docuisse, illa ei proponendo quae sibi a Deo fuissent ostensa. Quandoquidem facultates divinae non ideo collatae sunt, ut occulte delitescant, sed ut communem Ecclesiae aedificationem promoveant. Non tamen hinc sit, ut quod peculiari quodam privilegio Deus agit, id sit a nobis in exemplum trahendum.'

Chap. 2 n.115
St Peter Canisius, *De Maria Virgine*, II.1, p. 106: 'virgo non sterilis, sed foecunda: homini nupta, sed Dei plena: habens filium, sed nesciens virum: semper clausa, nec tamen prole destitua. Virgo sine corruptione gravida, et in partu inviolata. Virgo ante coniugium, virgo in coniugio, virgo praegnans, virgo lactans, virgo perpetua. Virgo sine libidine, concipiens Emanuelem. Virgo sine onere gestans uterum, sine dolore pariens Deum . . .'

ETHICS, POLITICS, SOCIAL WRITINGS
Chap. 4 n.69
Case, *Sphaera civitatis*, Oxford, 1588, I.3, p. 33: 'natura faeminam saepe solertem, industria literatam, educatio piam, experientia sapientem facit; quid obstat igitur, quo minus administret rempublicam? Iterum natura eam saepe liberam parit, cur serviret? Eam regni haeredem parit, cur non regeret? Haec piae leges, haec gentium mores, haec instituta patrum, haec sacrarum literarum exempla probant.'

LAW
Chap. 5 n.8
Cujas, *Opera omnia*, Lyons, 1606, IV, col. 1484: 'Imperatores capite puniendum censent eum qui infantem occiderit. *l. pen. Cod. ad legem Corn. de Sicar*. Qua poena etiam plectitur, qui virum occiderit. Homicidas enim lex ultore ferro persequitur. De infante dubitari poterat, quoniam lex Cornelia ait, qui hominem occiderit, et inde crimini nomen, Homicidium sive ἀνδροκτἄσία. Infans homo nondum est. Foemina item proprie non est homo *l. si quis aliquid abortionis D. de poenis*. Sed ut in lege Julia et Papia hominis significatio augetur a Jurisconsultis *leg. hominis D. de verborum significat.* ita et in lege Cornelia, ut foeminam quoque demonstret . . .'

Chap. 5 n.35
Tiraqueau, *Opera omnia*, II.1: 'dès que homme et femme, soyent nobles ou roturiers, sont mariez ensemble au pais de Poictou, par la coustume d'iceluy, la femme est en pouvoir de son mary, et n'est plus en pouvoir de son père, si l'avoit. Et ne peut valablement contracter, sans le consentement exprès de son mary, durant leur mariage, ne administrer les biens communs d'entre eux, ne les siens propres, sans l'auctorité et consentement de son dict mary.'

Chap. 5 n.56

Agrippa, *De nobilitate et praecellentia foeminei sexus . . . declamatio*, Antwerp, 1529, C7: 'sed virorum nimia tyrannide, contra divinum ius, naturaeque leges praevalente, data mulieribus libertas, iam, inquis, legibus interdicitur, consuetudine usuque aboletur, educatione extinguitur. Mulier namque mox ut nata est, a primis annis domi detinetur in desidia, ac velut altioris provinciae incapax, nihil praeter acus et filium concipere permittitur. Ubi exinde pubertatis annos attigerit, in mariti traditur zelotypum imperium, aut vestialium ergastulo perpetuo recluditur. Publica quaeque officia legibus sibi interdicta sunt. Postulare in iudicio licet prudentissima non permittitur, repelluntur praeterea in iurisdictione, in arbitrio, in adoptione, in intercessione, in procuratione, in tutela, in cura, in testamentaria et criminali causa . . .'

CONCLUSION
Chap. 6 n.22

Galileo, *Dialogo sopra i due massimi sistemi del mondo*, in *Opere*, ed. F. Flora, Milan and Naples, 1953, 1.412–13: 'io sono nel cuore al signor Simplicio, e veggio che e' si sente muovere assai dalla forza di queste pur troppo concludenti ragioni; ma, dall'altra banda, il vedere la grande autorità che si è acquistata Aristotile appresso l'universale, il considerare il numero de gli interpreti famosi che si sono affaticati per esplicare i suoi sensi, il vedere altre scienze, tanto utili e necessarie al publico, fondar gran parte della stima e reputazion loro sopra il credito d'Aristotile, lo confonde e spaventa assai; e me lo par sentir dire: "E a chi si ha da ricorrere per definire le nostre controversie, levato che fusse di seggio Aristotile? qual altro autore si ha da seguitare nelle scuole, nelle accademie, nelli studi? qual filosofo ha scritto tutte le parti della natural filosofia, e tanto ordinatamente, senza lasciar indietro pur una particolar conclusione? adunque si deve desolar quella fabbrica, sotto la quale si ricuoprono tanti viatori? si deve estrugger quell'asilo, quel Pritaneo, dove tanto agiatamente si ricoverano tanti studiosi, dove, senza esporsi all'ingiurie dell'aria, col solo rivoltar poche carte, si acquistano tutte le cognizioni della natura? si ha da spiantar quel propugnacolo, dove contro ad ogni nimico assalto in sicurezza si dimora?" Io gli compatisco, non meno che a quel signore che, con gran tempo, con spesa immensa, con l'opera di cento e cento artefici, fabbricò nobilissimo palazzo, e poi lo vegga, per esser stato mal fondato, minacciar rovina, e che, per non vedere con tanto cordoglio disfatte le mura di tante vaghe pitture adornate, cadute le colonne sostegni delle superbe logge, caduti i palchi dorati, rovinati gli stipiti, i frontespizi e le cornici marmoree con tanta spesa condotte, cerchi con catene, puntelli, contrafforti, barbacani e sorgozzoni di riparare alla rovina.'

Notes

CHAPTER 1

1 *Woman triumphant: feminism in French literature, 1610–52.* Oxford, 1977.
2 See, for example, D. *Thomae Aquinatis in Metaphysicorum Aristotelis Libros praeclarissima commentaria. . .cum defensionibus F. Bartholomaei Spinae super his commentariis. . .*, Venice, 1560, fo. 11r–v, for Aquinas's medieval paraphrase and Spina's Renaissance commentary.
3 See W. J. Ong, *Ramus, method and the decay of dialogue*, New York, 1974, pp. 199ff. Ong points out that dichotomies are not uniquely neoplatonic in origin. See also K. J. Höltgen, 'Synoptische Tabellen in der medizinischen Literatur und die Logik Agricolas und Ramus', *Sudhoffs Archiv*, XLIX (1965), 371–90.
4 For the anthropological and ancient background, see Lloyd, *Polarity and analogy*, pp. 15–171.
5 *In duos Aristotelis Libros Posteriores Analyticos commentarii* (1582), in *Opera logica*, Frankfurt, 1608, I.669–70; *Tabulae logicae* (1579), in *Opera logica*, II.127.
6 *Polarity and analogy*, pp. 51–5.
7 For a brief history of these terms, see Q. Breen, 'The terms loci communes and loci in Melanchthon', *Church history*, XVI (1947), 197–209, esp. 197–202.
8 See M. Foucault, *Les mots et les choses*, Paris, 1966, pp. 92ff.

CHAPTER 2

1 e.g. Johann Gerhard (1582–1637), *Loci theologici*, Jena, 1610–22. See also *The Cambridge history of the Bible*, ed. P. R. Ackroyd, C. F. Evans, G. W. H. Lampe and S. L. Greenslade, Cambridge, 1963–70, III.78; B. G. Armstrong, *Calvinism and the Amyraut heresy. Protestant scholasticism and humanism in seventeenth-century France*, Madison, 1969, esp. pp. 127–40; O. Fatio, *Nihil pulchrius ordine, contribution à l'étude de l'établissement de la discipline ecclésiastique aux Pays-Bas; ou Lambert Daneau aux Pays-Bas, 1581–1583*, Leyden, 1971.
2 See *The Cambridge history of the Bible*, III.79–93, 213–17.
3 e.g. Filippo Diez, *Summa praedicantium*, Lyons, 1592; Jean Dadré (*c.* 1550–1617?), *Loci communes similium et dissimilium*, Cologne, 1603 (both favourable to women); Luis de Granada (1504–88), *Sylva locorum communium*, Lyons, 1586; Antoine de Balinghem (1571–1630), *Scriptura sacra in locos communes digesta*, 2 vols., Douai, 1621 (both hostile to women).
4 See Beryl Smalley, *The study of the Bible in the Middle Ages*, Oxford, 1952, esp. pp. 247ff; H. de Lubac, *Exégèse médiévale, les quatre sens de l'Ecriture*, 2 pts in 4 vols., Paris, 1959–64.
5 *Commentarii in Proverbia Salomonis*, Paris, 1635, pp. 517ff.
6 See his sermon on the beheading of John the Baptist (*PG*, LIX.485ff).
7 As, for example, by Théophile Raynaud (1583?–1663), *Dissertatio de sobria alterius sexus frequentatione*, Lyons, 1653, p. 76: 'S. Chrysostomus. . .agnoscit mulierem et ad bonum et ad malum posse quamplurimum'.
8 *Physics*, I.9 [192a 22]; *De generatione animalium*, I.20 [729a 25ff]; *Historia animalium*, IX.1 [608a 21ff].

9 Cf. *De generatione animalium*, II.1 [731*b* 18ff]; on the relationship between the intention of nature and necessity, see *Physics*, II.8–9 [198*b* 10ff], and below, 3.9.4.

10 For a full account of Aquinas's and Albertus Magnus's understanding of Aristotle on this topic, see A. Mitterer, 'Mas occasionatus oder zwei Methoden der Thomas-deutung', *Zeitschrift für katholische Theologie*, LXXII (1950), 80–103.

11 *Summa theologica*, 1*a* 92,1.

12 *Commentarii in quinque Mosaicos libros*, Paris, 1539, p. 25; quoted without comment by Jean de la Haye (1593–1661), *Arbor vitae concionatorum cuius radix liber Geneseos*, Paris, 1633, p. 245; refuted by Benedictus Pererus, *Commentarii et disputationes in Genesim*, Cologne, 1601, pp. 212–14.

13 See, for example, Nicholas of Lyra (*c.* 1270–1340), *Postillae perpetuae*, in *Textus Biblie cum glosa ordinaria, Nicolai de Lyra postilla moralitatibus eiusdem*..., Basle, 1580, VI.221v; Aquinas, *Summa*, 2*a* 2*ae* 82,3; and below, 2.11.1.

14 e.g. De la Haye, *Arbor vitae concionatorum*, p. 237.

15 *Werke. Kritische Gesamtausgabe*, Weimar, 1883– , XLII.53. This is reminiscent of the possibly facetious feminist argument *ex ordine* (see below, 6.5.1).

16 *Ibid.*, XLII.51–2. Plutarch (*Conjugalia praecepta*, IX) has the same parallel sun/man moon/woman, with a rather different bias.

17 See Nicholas of Lyra, *Postillae perpetuae*, in *Textus Biblie*, 1.28v; Alphonsus Tostatus (*c.* 1414–54), *Opera omnia*, Venice, 1596, 1.17r. The source of this belief is the pseudo-Aristotelian *Physiognomia* (see P. Diepgen, 'Die Lehre von der leibseelischen Konstitution und die spezielle Anatomie und Physiognomie der Frau im Mittelalter', *Scientia*, LXXXIV (1949), 55).

18 *Tischreden*, no. 55, Weimar, 1912–21, 1.19: 'viri habent lata pectora et parva femora, ideo habent sapientiam. Mulieres habent angusta pectora et lata femora. Mulier debet esse οἰκουρός; id creatio indicat, habent enim latum podicem et femora, das sie sollen still sizen.'

19 e.g. André Valladier (1570–1638), *La saincte philosophie de l'âme*, Paris, 1614, pp. 818–19; François Dinet, *Le théâtre françois, des seigneurs et dames illustres*, Paris, 1642, II.2.

20 See *The Cambridge history of the Bible*, III.15.

21 'Agens semper patiente honorabilius' (Aristotle, *De anima*, III.5 [430*a* 17]); quoted by St Augustine, *De Genesi ad litteram*, XII.16, *PL*, XXXIV.467, and Aquinas, *Summa*, 1*a* 92,1.

22 *Summa theologica* (1*a* 2*ae*, inq. 4 tract. 2 sect. 2 q. 2 cap. 5; II.85.5), Quaracchi, 1924–48, II.627–8.

23 *In libros Sententiarum expositiones*, III.12 art. 3 q. 1, in *Opera omnia selecta*, Florence, 1941, III.264.

24 *Postillae perpetuae*, in *Textus Biblie*, VI.49r. The three reasons in common with Alexander of Hales and Bonaventura are passivity, imperfect nature and anagogical meaning.

25 Calvin, *Commentarius in Genesin*, in *Opera*, Brunswick, 1863– , XXIII.72; Peter Martyr Vermigli (1500–62), *Loci communes*, II.8.4, Heidelberg, 1622 (first edn 1576), pp. 191–2.

26 *In omnes divi Pauli epistolas commentaria*, Paris, 1638, pp. 284–5.

27 *De veritate*, 5,9 d.9, quoted by Mitterer, *Zeitschrift für katholische Theologie*, LXXII.98: 'nisi ergo esset aliqua virtus quae intenderet femineum sexum, generatio feminae esset omnino a casu, sicut et aliorum monstrorum'.

28 The question of monstrosity arises also in connection with the debate about Eve's 'other matter' (a rib would not be sufficient to account for all her body): see *Textus Biblie*, 1.38v–43r; Aquinas, *Summa*, 1*a* 92,3.

29 *De Genesi ad litteram*, III.22, *PL*, XXXIV.294; Aquinas, *Summa*, 1*a* 93,4.

30 See W. Pagel, *Das medizinische Weltbild des Paracelsus*, Wiesbaden, 1962, pp. 62–70; Petrus Calanna (1531–1606), *Philosophia seniorum sacerdotia et platonica*, Palermo, 1599, p. 173.

31 The report by Gregory of Tours of an unnamed bishop's proposition at the second Council of Mâcon (585); see *Histoire des conciles*, ed. H. Leclercq, Paris, 1909, III.1, 211–12.

32 *Epistolae*, ed. Christianus Acidalius, Hanau, 1606, p. 39.

33 Notably Simon Gediccus, whose refutation full of scatalogical abuse appears at Leipzig in 1595; when the *Disputatio nova* is published together with his reply, it appears with the

title *Disputatio perjucunda qua anonymus probare nititur mulieres homines non esse: cui opposita est Simonis Gedicci. . .defensio sexus muliebris.*

34 e.g. J. P. Lotz, *Gynaicologia*, Rintheln, 1630; J. U. Wolff, *Discursus: de foeminarum in jure civili et canonico privilegiis, immunitatibus et praeeminentia*, Rostock, 1615.

35 Thomas Nashe (?), *An almond for a parrat* (1590), in *Works*, ed. R. B. McKerrow and F. P. Wilson, Oxford, 1958, III.348.

36 *Iuvenilia* (London, 1633: facsimile reprint Amsterdam, 1970), G 2v–3v (*Problemes*, VI: 'Why hath the common opinion afforded women soules?').

37 The German title is *Gründ und probierliche Beschreibung/Argument und Schluss-Articul, sampt beygefügten aussführlichen Beantwortungen: Belangend die Frag/ ob die Weiber Menschen sein/ oder nicht?*

38 See *Dictionnaire historique et critique*, s.v. Acidalius and Gediccus; Vossius, *De origine idololatriae*, III.48, in *Opera omnia*, Amsterdam, 1700, V.361–2.

39 *De Genesi ad litteram*, XII.42, *PL*, XXXIV.452; Aquinas, *Summa*, 1a 93.4. Gerhard refers to 'disputationes quaedam veterum' on this subject which predate Augustine's text (*Loci theologici*, II.202–3).

40 'Le statut de la femme en droit canonique médiéval', in *La Femme* (Recueils de la société Jean Bodin, XII), Brussels, 1962, II.80–2.

41 XII.7, *PL*, XLII.1003–5.

42 *Quaestiones celeberrimae in Genesim*, Paris, 1623, cols. 1051–4. This work was written to refute Francesco Giorgio's *In Scripturam sacram problemata* (Paris, 1574, republished 1622).

43 *Loci theologici*, II.202–3; N. Selneccerus, *In Genesim commentarius*, Leipzig, 1569, p. 115.

44 *Loci communes*, I.12, p. 64.

45 See Maclean, *Feminism in French literature*, p. 41.

46 See P. D. Huet, *Origeniana* (1668), ed. J. P. Migne, *PG*, XVII.991 for a summary bibliography.

47 XXII.17, *PL*, XLI.778.

48 *In libros Sententiarum expositiones*, IV.44, *Opera theologica selecta*, IV.908–9.

49 *Summa*, Suppl. 81,3.

50 'Quisquis ergo vir est in Christo, ille demum omni ex parte est absolutus' (*Commentarii in epistolas ad Ephesios*, in *Opera*, LI.200); see also Conrad Pellikan (1478–1556), *In omnes apostolicas epistolas commentaria*, Zürich, 1539, p. 383.

51 Gerhard, *Loci theologici*, VIII.853–5; Cornelius a Lapide, *In omnes Pauli epistolas*, pp. 509–10; Wolfgang Musculus (Mosel) (1497–1563), *In epistolas Pauli ad Galatas et Ephesios commentarii*, Basle, 1599, II.108.

52 Gerhard, *Loci theologici*, VIII.853–4: 'inter scholasticos Scotus 2 *Sent. dist.* 20 expresse docet, *omnes foeminas excepta sola B Virgine, in sexu virili resurrecturas. 1. quia sexus foemineus est accidens et imperfectio hominis, iam vero in resurrectione omnis imperfectio abolebitur. 2. quia foemina est mas occasionatus teste Philosophi, unde in foemina producenda errasse Natura, ut cum vellet producere hominem perfectum marem scilicet, deficiente virtute generativa seminis pro mare produxerit foeminam'*. Cornelius a Lapide, *In omnes Pauli epistolas*, pp. 509–10, has exactly the same text.

53 *Opera omnia*, I.228–39.

54 Duns Scotus, *In quatuor libros Sententiarum quaestiones*, ed. Hugo Cavellus, Antwerp, 1620, p. 228; *idem*, *Opera omnia*, ed. Franciscus Lychetus, Lyons, 1639, VI.2, 824–5.

55 e.g. Valladier, *La saincte philosophie de l'âme*, pp. 818–19.

56 Gerhard, *Loci theologici*, VIII.854–5; Cornelius a Lapide, *In omnes Pauli epistolas*, pp. 510–11. Gerhard follows Luther in rejecting the argument from *mas occasionatus*; Cornelius a Lapide accepts it, but adds a eulogy of woman as a rider, cf. above, 2.3.2).

57 *Sententiae*, II.20; Aquinas, *Summa*, 2a 2ae 163,4; 165,2; Tertullian, *De cultu mulierum*, I.1, *PL*, I.1305; also 1 Tim. 2: 14.

58 *Loci communes*, II.11, pp. 255–6.

59 *Epistolae*, CXXVIII, *PL*, XXII.1096.

60 *Summa*, 2a 2ae 169,2.

61 *Introduction à la vie dévote*, III.25, in *Œuvres*, ed. A. Ravier and R. Devos, Paris, 1969, pp. 202–4.

62 For a summary bibliography of French tracts on this subject, see Maclean, *Feminism in French literature*, pp. 70–1, 134–5.

63 *Sermons sur la première à Thimothée*, XVII, in *Opera*, LIII.205–6.

64 *Summa*, Venice, 1503, III.42–9; expanded by Alexis Trousset (alias Jacques Olivier), *Alphabet de l'imperfection et malice des femmes*, Paris, 1617.

65 See Maclean, *Feminism in French literature*, p. 31, for a summary bibliography.

66 See Tertullian, *De cultu mulierum*, I.I, *PL*, I.1419; Chrysostom, *Homiliae in Matthaeum*, XXXII, *PG*, LVI.803, often quoted in its Latin translation: 'quid autem est aliud mulier, nisi amicitiae inimica, ineffugabilis poena, necessarium malum, naturalis tentatio, desiderabilis calamitas, domesticum periculum, delectabile detrimentum, mali natura, boni colore depicta?'.

67 The biblical locus is Gen. 3:15. See Nicholas of Lyra, *Postillae perpetuae*, in *Textus Biblie*, I.42v; Tostatus, *Opera omnia*, I.21r. By analogy man is metaphorically associated with reason; therefore in marriage is found a figure for the subordination of the passions to man's rational nature (*Textus Biblie*, VI.49r). See also Aloysius Novarini, *Adagia ex sanctorum Patrum. . .prompta*, Lyons, 1637, pp. 86–8 on fire as an image for woman.

68 e.g. Matthieu Lambert (1540?–1602), *Discours du danger et péril qu'il y a de converser et hanter trop familiarement avec femmes, tant séculières que religieuses*, Liege, 1596.

69 The anecdote is retailed by André Du Chesne (1584–1640), *Figures mystiques du riche et précieux cabinet des dames*, Paris, 1605, fo. 51.

70 Louis Machon, *Discours ou sermon apologétique, en faveur des femmes*, Paris, 1641, pp. 34–5; for other feminist interpretations, see Maclean, *Feminism in French literature*, pp. 42–4.

71 St Peter Canisius (1521–97), *De Maria virgine incomparabili*, II.1, Ingolstadt, 1577, p. 108.

72 Franciscus Junius (Du Jon) (1545–1602), *Opera theologica*, Geneva, 1607, I.88: 'eas poenas quae viro impositae sunt, foeminae quoque communes esse: sed non contra, eas quae foeminae singulares sunt, cum viro communicari oportere'.

73 See *Textus Biblie*, I.235r–6r; I.241r. Man, too, can be polluted by his sexual nature (see Lev. 15:16–18, and Peter Martyr Vermigli, *Loci communes*, III.6, pp. 466–7).

74 e.g. William Whateley, *A Bride-bush* (1619), quoted by L. Carrive, 'Les puritains et la femme', in *La femme en Angleterre et dans les colonies américaines aux XVIIe et XVIIIe siècles* (*Actes du colloque de la société d'études angloaméricaines des XVIIe et XVIIIe siècles*), Lille, 1976, p. 61.

75 *Opera omnia*, VI, 46.

76 *Textus Biblie*, VI, 49.

77 *Commentarius in epistolas Pauli ad Corinthios I*, in *Opera*, XLIX.476.

78 Peter Martyr Vermigli, *Loci communes*, IV.1, pp. 588–9; the biblical *locus* is 1 Tim. 2:14.

79 See Metz, 'Le statut de la femme en droit canonique médiéval', in *La Femme*, II.99–100. Midwives may however administer the sacrament of baptism to newborn infants in the absence of a priest, if there is a serious danger that the infant might die. Aquinas (*Summa*, Suppl. 39,1) discusses this exclusion from orders; to the arguments that women can be prophetesses (see below, 2.11.1) and can have precedence as abbesses, he replies that prophecy is a gift of God, not a sacrament, and that abbesses have only temporal powers. While agreeing that the sacramental character is in the soul which has no sex, he points out that males are more suitable to be priests 'ex necessitate' ('in sexu foemineo non potest significari aliqua eminentia gradus, quia mulier statum subjectionis habet'), and 'ex necessitate praecepti, propter congruitatem ad sacramentum'. The first argument is based on the distinction of *res* and *significatio rei*, which recalls both the four levels of meaning in Scripture, and the distinction of *res* and *verbum* in Roman Law (see below, 5.1.6). For discussion of the nature of sacramental character, see Augustine, *Sermo* 71.19.32, *PL*, XXXVIII.462 and *Contra epistolam Parmeniani*, 2.13.9, *PL*, XLIII.71.

80 See Metz, 'Le statut de la femme en droit canonique médiéval', in *La Femme*, II.100. For a sympathetic account of the special powers of abbesses, see Etienne d'Alvin (b. 1565), *Tractatus de potestate episcoporum, abbatum. . .nec non abbatissarum*, Paris, 1607, fos. 1ff.

81 See William Tyndale, *An answer to Sir Thomas More's dialogue* (1531), quoted by Carrive, in *La femme en Angleterre*, p. 66, who also gives a list of puritan texts which approve of preaching by women.

82 *Textus Biblie*, VI.49; Tostatus, *Opera omnia*, I.146ff. See also Calvin, *Opera*, XXIII.72;

Peter Martyr Vermigli, *Loci communes*, II.8, pp. 191–2.

83 See Carrive, in *La femme en Angleterre*, pp. 63–4; Marguerite de Valois (1552–1615), *Lettre à François Loyrot*, quoted by Maclean, *Feminism in French literature*, p. 42.

84 See Cornelius a Lapide, *In omnes Pauli epistolas*, p. 534; Calvin, *Commentarius in epistolas Pauli ad Ephesios*, in *Opera omnia theologica*, Geneva, 1617, V.3, p. 753.

85 *Contra Faustum*, XXII.31, *PL*, XLII.420.

86 *Postillae perpetuae*, in *Textus Biblie*, 1.355v: 'per hoc significatur (Deut. 22:5 'non induetur mulier veste virili, nec vir utetur veste feminea') quod mulier exercere non debet actus viriles ut praedicare, docere et similia; nec vir actus muliebres, ut filare, et lavare pannos et similia'.

87 Aquinas, *Summa*, 1a 92,2; *Textus Biblie*, 1.39r; Musculus, *In Mosis Genesim plenissimi commentarii*, Basle, 1565, p. 75.

88 Cornelius a Lapide, *In Pentateuchum Mosis commentaria*, Paris, 1637, p. 81; Pierre Du Moulin (1568–1658), *Première decade de sermons*, Geneva, 1642, pp. 116–53 (a sermon on Col. 3:19).

89 See Carrive, in *La femme en Angleterre*, pp. 61–2.

90 On Renaissance attitudes to marriage, see M. A. Screech, *The Rabelaisian marriage*, London, 1958, pp. 66–83, 104–25.

91 See Carrive, in *La femme en Angleterre*, pp. 62–3.

92 On exceptions not proving rules, see Peter Martyr Vermigli, *Loci communes*, IV.1, pp. 588–9, quoted below, 2.11.1.

93 *Paedagogus*, 1.4, *PG*, VIII.259–62.

94 Erasmus, Paraclesis, in *Opera omnia*, Leyden, 1703–6, V.140; Vives, *De institutione foeminae Christianae*, Antwerp, 1524, 1.3, C3rff.

95 See K. V. Thomas, 'Women and the Civil War Sects', *Past and present*, XIII (1958), 42–62; N. Z. Davis, *Society and culture in early modern France*, London, 1975, pp. 78ff, who examines also the emancipatory effect of Bible reading and freedom from the influence of the priest on women.

96 *De hominis structura*, 1.22, *PG*, XXX.34–5; for use of this argument, see Simon Majolus (fl. 1572–97), *Colloquia physica* (1597), Mainz, 1615, 1.3, p. 47; Nicolas L'Archevesque, *Les grandeurs sur-eminentes de la très-saincte Vierge Marie*, Paris, 1638, pp. 485–6; Jacques Du Bosc, *La femme heroïque*, Paris, 1645, 1.29. It is striking that the Alexandrian Fathers are explicitly favourable to woman (see also Theodoret, *PG*, LXXXIII.836), and that this attitude is linked to a belief that there is no sex in heaven (see Huet, *Origeniana*, in *PG*, XVII.991).

97 Biblical *loci* are Prov. 31:10–29; Ecclus. 36:27

98 One of the 'commemorationes communes quando non dicitur ejus officium parvum'.

99 *Postillae perpetuae*, in *Textus Biblie*, III.636r.

100 *Summa*, 2a 2ae 83,3. A similar idea, applied to the 'esprits simples' is found in the secular moralist Michel de Montaigne (*Essais*, ed. A. Thibaudet and M. Rat, Paris, 1962, 1.54, p. 299).

101 See Judges 4:4; Luke 1:42–6, 2:36; also Exod. 15:20; 1 Sam. 2:1.

102 *Textus Biblie*, VI.56v; Aquinas, *Summa*, Suppl. 39,1.

103 *Loci communes*, IV.1, pp. 588–9; see also 1.4, pp. 6–7.

104 See E. Wind, *Pagan mysteries of the Renaissance*, London, 1967, pp. 175, 242.

105 e.g. Luke 1:53; 1 Cor. 1:27; 2 Cor. 2:9; and examples such as Judith (9:15–16) and David (1 Sam. 17:20–55). Renaissance writers sometimes pay tribute to powerful women by reference to this commonplace: e.g. Peter Martyr Vermigli, *Epistolae*, XXXVI, in *Loci communes*, p. 889.

106 *Carmina*, LXXXVI, LXXXVII, LXXXVIII, XCI, *PL*, CLXXVIII.1811–15.

107 Bonaventura, *Opera theologica selecta*, III.264; Nicholas of Lyra, *Postillae perpetuae*, in *Textus Biblie*, II.35v.

108 For examples taken from French texts, see Maclean, *Feminism in French literature*, pp. 73ff.

109 A patristic commonplace; see Augustine, *De vera religione*, XXXVIII, *PL*, XXXIV.153, and *Sermones ad fratres in eremo*, XLII, *PL*, XL.1316.

110 See H. Bremond, *Histoire littéraire du sentiment religieux en France*, Paris, 1930, II.

111 For a fuller account of this theory, see M. A. Screech, 'The illusion of Postel's feminism', *Journal of the Warburg and Courtauld Institutes*, XVI (1953), 162–70.
112 See Pagel, *Das medizinische Weltbild des Paracelsus*, pp. 62–70.
113 See David Lagneus, *Harmonia seu consensus philosophorum chemicorum*, in *Theatrum chemicum*, Strasbourg, 1659, IV.724. This is only one of many such schemata; see J. Read, *Prelude to chemistry*, London, 1939, pp. 27ff, 101ff.
114 See Balinghem, *Scriptura sacra in locos communes digesta*, 1.539–85; Cornelius a Lapide, *Commentarii in Proverbia Salomonis*, pp. 521ff, which is very rich in figurative interpretations of this passage. St Bernard of Clairvaux, *Homilia in Lucam* 1:26–7, *PL*, CLXXXIII.63, is the principal scholastic source for this association.
115 *De Maria Virgine*, II.1, p. 106.
116 e.g. Heinrich Kornmann, *Sibylla TrygAndriana, seu de virginitate, virginum statu et iure tractatus novus et iucundus*, Frankfurt, 1610, which contains, as well as facetious speculations, serious commentary on legal topics and an account of mystical powers. On the use of *iucundus* in the title, see below, 6.2.2.
117 See Carrive, in *La femme en Angleterre*, pp. 61–2.
118 See Wind, *Pagan mysteries*, pp. 75ff; E. H. Gombrich, *Symbolic images: studies in the art of the Renaissance*, London, 1972, pp. 66ff.
119 For a fuller account of neoplatonist theories, see Jean Festugière, *La philosophie de l'amour de Marsile Ficin et son influence sur la littérature française au XVIe siècle*, Paris, 1941.
120 *Stromata*, *PG*, IX.23–4.
121 See also R. V. Merrill and R. J. Clements, *Platonism in French Renaissance poetry*, New York, 1957, pp. 99–117.
122 *In Plotinum*, 'De providentia primum', 11, in *Opera omnia*, Paris, 1641, II.645.
123 *Epistolae*, in *Opera omnia*, 1.721.
124 *Ibid.* 1.722. On this use of vocabulary, see below, 4.4.2.
125 *The crowne coniugall*, Middelburgh, 1620, pp. 12–13.
126 See Carrive, in *La femme en Angleterre*, pp. 62–3.
127 See Thomas, *Past and present*, XIII.42–62.
128 For an account of early Reformation strategies of resolving textual inconsistencies, see *The Cambridge history of the Bible*, III.12ff.

CHAPTER 3

1 *Die Zeugungs- und Vererbungslehre der Antike und ihr Nachwirken* (Abhandlungen der Geistes- und Sozialwissenschaftlichen Klasse, LXX (1950)), Wiesbaden, 1951.
2 *Marcello Malpighi and the evolution of embryology*, Ithaca, New York, 1966, II.752ff.
3 *Ibid.* II.754.
4 e.g. by Girolamo Mercuriale (1530–1606), *De morbis muliebribus* (1582), II.2, in *Gynaecea*, ed. Israel Spachius, Strasbourg, 1597, pp. 230–1.
5 See Adelmann, *Marcello Malpighi*, II.755.
6 *De universa mulierum medicina* (1603), Hamburg, 1662, 1.19: 'una cum praestanti doctrina, similes fabellos et prodigiosa multa contineri, quae facile possint tyronibus fucum facere'.
7 Its editors are, respectively, Hans Kaspar Wolf, Gaspard Bauhin and Israel Spachius. Spachius's cumulative edition contains the following texts: Felix Platter (1536–1614), *De mulierum partibus generationis dicatis tabulae iconibus illustratae* (1583); Moschion, *De passionibus mulierum* (sixth cent. A.D.), ed. Konrad Gesner and Hans Kaspar Wolf; Trotula, *Muliebria* (eleventh cent.); Nicolas de la Roche (Rocheus), *De morbis mulierum curandis* (1542); Luigi Bonacciuoli (Buonaccioli, Bonaciolus) (d. c. 1540), *Enneas muliebris* (c. 1480); Jacques Dubois (Sylvius) (1478–1555), *De mensibus mulierum et hominis generatione* (1555); Jakob Rüff (Ruffus) (1500–58), *De conceptu et generatione hominis* (1554); Mercuriale, *De morbis muliebribus*; Giovanni Battista da Monte (Montanus) (1498–1551), *De affectibus uterinis libellus, cum decem consiliis muliebribus* (1554); Vittore Trincavelli (1496–1568), *Consilia muliebria tria* (1586); Albertino Bottoni (d. c. 1596), *De morbis muliebribus* (1585); Jean Le Bon (d. c. 1583), *Therapia puerperarum* (1571); Ambroise Paré (1510?–90), *De hominis generatione* (1573); Albucasis, *De morbis*

muliebribus (eleventh cent.); François Rousset, *De partu caesareo* (1581), trans. Gaspard Bauhin; Bauhin (1560–1624), *Libellus variarum historiarum ea quae in libro de partu caesareo tractantur comprobantium* (1588); Maurice de la Corde (Cordaeus) (fl. 1569–74), *Commentarii in librum priorem Hippocratis de muliebribus* (1585); Martinus Akakia (1539–88), *De morbis muliebribus* (1597); Luis Mercado (Mercatus) (1525?–1611), *De mulierum affectionibus* (1579). I have included dates of birth and death where known in order to indicate that many works were published posthumously, although probably known during their authors' lifetime (cf. La Corde, below, 3.3.7). The dates following the title are those of the earliest recorded editions in Hirsch or Durling. *Gynaecea* is hereafter referred to as *G*, and the book and chapter number of the author's work alone are given.

8   e.g. by Mercado, 1.2, *G*, 805,807, who refers to *Summa*, 1*a*92,1 and *Summa contra gentiles*, XCV. See above, 2.2.2.

9   Notably Mercado, 1.1, *G*, 803–8; Mercuriale, 1.1, *G*, 209; Akakia, prolegomena, *G*, 745; Jean Varandal (Varandaeus) (d. 1617), *Tractatus therapeuticus de morbis mulierum* (1619), preface, in *Opera omnia*, Lyons, 1658, pp. 477–81; de Castro, *De universa mulierum medicina*, 1.126–31; André Du Laurens (Laurentius), *Anatomica humani corporis historia* (1593), VIII, cap. 1, Frankfurt, 1600, p. 280.

10 Adelmann, *Marcello Malpighi*, II.757.

11 *Ad libram Fernelii de procreatione hominis commentarius*, Paris, 1578, fo. 17v, quoted by Adelmann, *Marcello Malpighi*, II.753: 'cum ergo stultum sit ratione pugnare contra sensum et experientiam, pro antiquitatis reverentia'.

12 Reinier de Graaf, *De mulierum organis generatione inservientibus tractatus novus*, Leyden, 1672; on Karl Ernst von Baer, see Lesky, *Die Zeugungs-und Vererbungslehre*, p. 149.

13 *De generatione animalium*, 1.2 [716*a* 13]. Usually rendered into Latin as 'feminam in seipso, marem in alio gignere'. This is universally accepted ('ex confessa omnium hominum opinione', Kaspar Hofmann, *De generatione hominis*, Frankfurt, 1629, p. 2).

14 This commonplace from *Physics*, 1.9 [192*a* 22] is elegantly rendered by Gabriele Falloppio (1523–62), *Tractatus de metallis seu fossilibus*, XI, in *Opera omnia*, Frankfurt, 1600, 1.300: 'ea proportio quae est inter materiam et formam, est inter foeminam et marem. Nam foemina sustentatur mari, et appetit marem, tanquam perfectionem, quemadmodum et materia appetit formam, tanquam optatum et amatum'.

15 *Scientia*, LXXXIV, 53–8, 132–4.

16 See O. Temkin, *Galenism: rise and decline of a medical philosophy*, Cornell, 1973, p. 79; P. Diepgen, *Frau und Frauenheilkunde in der Kultur des Mittelalters*, Stuttgart, 1963, pp. 147–8. See also below, 3.4.1.

17 The theory of the humours is attributed by Aristotle to Empedocles (*Metaphysics*, A.6 [981*a* 25f]). Galen develops it in *De elementis*, II.1 (see da Monte, 'doctrina de quatuor humoribus', in *Medicina universa*, ed. M. Weinrich, Frankfurt, 1587, pp. 159–61).

18 On monsters and monstrosity, see Paré, *Des monstres et prodiges* (1573), ed. J. Céard, Geneva, 1971; Martin Weinrich (1548–1609), *De ortu monstruorum commentarius*, (Breslau), 1595.

19 1.9 [1058*a* 31–2], usually latinized as 'mas et femina non differunt specie'.

20 'Plato dubitare videtur, utro in genere ponat mulierem, rationalium animantium an brutorum', *Opera omnia*, IV.418. Giovanni Nevizzano attributes this dictum to Eusebius, *De praeparatione evangelica*, XII.12, but I have not been able to find it there (see *Sylvae nuptialis libri sex* (1521), Lyons, 1556, p. 22). Among satirical texts which refer to this quotation are Jacques Yver, *Le printemps*, Paris, 1572, fos. 102–3; anon. *Disputatio nova contra mulieres*, XLIII; Giuseppe Passi, *I donneschi diffetti*, Venice, 1599, p. 8; Trousset-Olivier, *Alphabet*, p. 418.

21 Referred to by Tiraqueau, *De legibus connubialibus*, 1.1.55, in *Opera omnia*, Frankfurt, 1616, II.12; Montaigne, *Essais*, ed. Thibaudet and Rat, III.5, p. 834; Pierre Grégoire, *De republica*, Frankfurt, 1597, VII.11, p. 446; Paolo Zacchias (1584–1659), *Quaestiones medicolegales* (1624–50), Amsterdam, 1651, p. 470.

22 e.g. by Joachimus Eberartus, *Bonus mulier*, n.p., 1616, E3v, who assumes that Scaliger's *Exercitatio cxxxi* (see below, 3.7.3) was written 'contra Cujatium' (see below, 5.2.1), and Johann Peter Lotz (Lotichius) (1598–1669), *Gynaecologia*, Rintheln, 1630, p. 30, who

attributes the *Disputatio nova contra mulieres* to Cujas.

23 For an exemplary text, see Weinrich, *De ortu monstruorum*, II.65–9.

24 e.g. Akakia, prolegomena, G, 745.

25 e.g. Bartholomäus Keckermann, *Systema physicum*, Hanau, 1617, pp. 593–601.

26 *De generatione animalium*, II.3 [737a 27]; *De usu partium corporis*, XIV.6.

27 Lyons, 1588, pp. 50–8.

28 1.32–3, Frankfurt, 1605, pp. 210–12.

29 Hanau, 1617, pp. 572–3.

30 Viz. Sebastian Meyer, *Augustae laudes Divinae Majestatis e divinis Galeni de usu partium libris selectae*, Freiburg, 1627, pp. 197–8.

31 On this point see de Valles, *In aphorismos Hippocratis commentarii* (1561), Cologne, 1589, p. 166.

32 *De generatione hominis*, pp. 3–4. The texts referred to by Hofmann are Hippocrates, *Aphorisms*, V.38,48,62; *Epidemics*, III.70, IV.45–6, VII.32; *Regimen*, I.22; Aristotle, *De partibus animalium*, III.1; *Historia animalium*, IV.11, V.10–11, VII.1, 4–5, 11, IX.1; *De generatione animalium*, I.19–20, II.3–6, IV.1–3, 7, V.3–4, IX.2; Galen, *De usu partium corporis*, XIV.1–6; *De semine*, II.1–5; *De caussis pulsuum*, III.2.

33 *De calido innato et semine pro Aristotele adversus Galenum*, Leyden, 1634, VII.4, pp. 214–15. For the parallel with plant life (male–seed/woman–earth) see Plato, *Timaeus*, 91D, and Aristotle, *De generatione animalium*, I.2 [716a 17]. Fortunio Liceti (1577–1657), *De perfecta constitutione hominis in utero*, Padua, 1616, XIII, p. 47, claims that to be the place of procreation is not ignoble, since all procreation is active (on activity being noble, see Chap. 2, n.21). Cremonini's views accord well with medieval discussions (e.g. Trotula, G, 42) and early Renaissance medicine (e.g. da Monte, 'De temperamentis ratione sexus', in *Medicina universa*, pp. 156–9).

34 *Observationes anatomicae*, in *Opera omnia*, pp. 420–2, cited by Du Laurens, *Anatomica humani corporis historia*, VII, cap. 12, p. 273, and Johann Schenk von Grafenberg (1530–1598), *Observationes medicae* (1584–97), Frankfurt, 1609, pp. 601–3.

35 A related question is that of sex change; see below, 3.5.4.

36 *Anatomica humani corporis historia*, VII, q. 8, pp. 274–5.

37 See P. Hoffmann, 'Féminisme cartésien', *Travaux de linguistique et de littérature*, VII.2 (1969), 83–105.

38 The *loci classici* compare these organs to the eyes of a mole: see Aristotle, *Historia animalium*, I.9 [491b 26], IV.8 [533a 10], where these eyes are said to represent a case of the natural course of development congenitally arrested, and especially Galen, *De usu partium corporis*, XIV.6, cited by Hofmann, *Commentarii in Galeni de usu partium corporis*, Frankfurt, 1625, p. 309, and Emilio Parisano (1567–1643), *De subtilitate*, Venice, 1623, pp. 147–8.

39 Parisano, *loc. cit.*: 'mulier seu foemina quatenus foemina perfecta est, nec perfectior esse potest: quoniam ad concipiendum, ad procreandam prolem, continendam, fovendam, aleandam, perficiendamque talibus instrumentis, talique temperatione opus habuit'; cf. Valladier, *La saincte philosophie de l'âme*, pp. 818–19.

40 II.6, in *Opera omnia*, Lyons, 1663, VI.645–54.

41 *Exercitationes*, CCLXXIV, Frankfurt, 1592, pp. 832–8: 'eundem viri, mulierisque calorem. In muliere non apparere, dilutum humore multo. In viro sentiri, quod acriatur siccitate'.

42 Scaliger is the editor of the *Historia animalium* and the peripatetic Theophrastus's *De causis plantarum* and the pseudo-Aristotelian *De plantis*. For his anti-feminist views, see *Electa Scaligerea, hoc est Julii Caesari Scaligeri sententiae, praecepta, definitiones, axiomata*, ed. Christophorus Freibisius, Hanau, 1634, pp. 308–13.

43 e.g. Akakia, G, 745; de Castro, *De universa mulierum medicina*, I.131.

44 G, 506–7; but La Corde (fl. 1569–74) argues that, according to Hippocrates, woman is hotter only in blood temperature.

45 *Prognosticorum Hippocratis è Graeco in Latinum versio, cum expositionibus in Galeni commentaria*, Lyons, 1576, p. 1143.

46 e.g. Du Laurens, *Anatomica humani corporis historia*, VIII, q. 2, p. 283.

47 Classical authorities records that, in some animals, the female is the hotter, viz. bears, leopards, lions and falcons (Aristotle, *Historia animalium*, IX.1 [608a 35]; Pliny, *Natural*

History, XI.110). According to de Valles (*Controversiae medicae*, I.9, pp. 27–9, quoting
Galen, *De caussis pulsuum*, III.2) this is because her function is different from that of the
human female, which is 'concipere, lactare et educare foetus'.

48 Tostatus, *Opera omnia*, I.232.

49 *De caussis pulsuum*, III.2; Giovanni Zecchi (1533–1601), *Tractatus de pulsibus* (1599),
Frankfurt, 1650, pp. 933–5; de Castro, *De universa mulierum medicina*, I.91–8. According
to Aristotelian taxonomy, this would still mean that in general men were hotter than
women, since the best of any class governs its relative position to other classes (see *Topics*,
III.2 [117b 32ff] and below, 4.5.3).

50 The *locus classicus* is in Macrobius, *Saturnalia*, VII.7.5, quoted by Mercuriale, G, 257.

51 See Chap. 3, n.32 for the sources of these *loci*.

52 Although also closely linked to the debates, the controversy concerning the origin and
concoction of semen is not relevant here, as it has no bearing on the difference of sex. For
an informed Renaissance account, see Du Laurens, *Anatomica humani corporis historia*, VIII,
q. 4, pp. 287–9.

53 According to Cajetan, the phrase 'caro de carne mea' indicates that woman does not
possess a *virtus formatrix*, but merely provides matter in procreation (*Commentarii in
quinque Mosaicos libros*, p. 25).

54 In the Aristotelian understanding of fertilization, only the male needs be aroused, as the
female does not contribute to the generation of the foetus; for Galen, sexual pleasure in
both male and female is functional (i.e. both woman and man must be aroused for them
to be fertile and emit semen). Some Galenists not only prescribe means of arousing
woman, but also go so far as to suggest that there is a further, non-functional, element in
sexual pleasure which softens man's sad lot on this earth ('mulieribus [maribusque]
videtur venerei coitus sensus à natura datus, non tantùm ad sobolis propagationem et
speciei humanae conservationem, sed etiam ad humanae vitae miserias, voluptatis illius
tanquam blandimentis leniendas et demulcendas': Paré, III, G, 405). The whole topic of
sexual pleasure in marriage (or outside it) is debated with varying degrees of obliquity
and varying degrees of austerity; the analogy most often made is that with the pleasures
of food and drink. Scaliger's aphorism 'sapientes bibunt ut ne bibant; nebulones bibunt
ut bibant' (paralleled by 'appetit foemina ut impleatur; mas ut depleatur', *Exercitationes*,
CXXXI.4, p. 454) may be placed at one end of the spectrum; Francisco Barbaro's
suggestion of moderate indulgence in sexual pleasure using the metaphor of eating and
gluttony ('De coitus ratione', in *De re uxoria* (fifteenth cent.), Amsterdam, 1639, pp.
141–8, cf. Aquinas, *Summa*, suppl. 49,1, followed by St Francis of Sales, *Introduction à la
vie dévote*, in *Œuvres*, ed. Ravier and Devos, pp. 240–4) may be placed at the other.
Between these views falls Michel de Montaigne's suggestion that sexual pleasure is to be
enjoyed with prostitutes and in illicit relationships, and dutiful but unpleasurable coitus
undertaken with the wife (*Essais*, ed. Thibaudet et Rat, I.30, pp. 197–8, and III.5, *passim*;
cf. Plutarch, *Conjugalia praecepta*, XVI).

55 e.g. Vesalius, *Humani corporis fabrica*, Basle, 1543, pp. 145, 520, 532, quoted by Screech,
The Rabelaisian marriage, p. 92, and W. Wiegand, 'What about the *Fabrica* of Vesalius?',
in *Three Vesalian essays*, New York, 1952, pp. 59–63.

56 *Opera omnia*, p. 421.

57 *Marcello Malpighi*, II.739.

58 *Exercitationes*, VI.7, pp. 33–5.

59 *De calido innato et semine, passim*.

60 *De perfecta constitutione hominis in utero*, XIII–XV, pp. 45–55.

61 *Physiologiae peripateticae libri sex* (1603), Geneva, 1629, V.15, pp. 428–40; pp. 437–8 are
plagiarized from Mercuriale (see G, 258), a Galenist.

62 Hofmann cites *De semine*, II.4 and *De usu partium corporis*, XIV.7 as Galenic *loci* which
negate the suggestion made in *De semine*, II.2 that woman possesses semen (*Apologiae pro
Galeno libri sex*, Lyons, 1668, I.189).

63 *Disputatio...in qua ea, quae de semine sunt controversa inter peripateticos et veteres medicos, et
doctissimos quosdam neotericos accurantissime discutuntur*, Treviso, 1609.

64 *Anatomica humani corporis historia*, VIII, q. 5, pp. 289–91.

65 There is a controversy about the origin of the *mola uteri*: see de Valles, *Controversiae*

medicae (1564), Frankfurt, 1582, II.6, p. 67; Mercuriale, 1.3, G, 219–22; Du Laurens, *Anatomica humani corporis historia*, VIII, q. 5, p. 291; de Castro, *De universa mulierum medicina*, I.45–8.

66 Vicenza, 1597, II.3, pp. 538–66.

67 IV.5, G, 273. The ancient theory derives from Empedocles according to Aristotle (*De generatione animalium*, 1.18 [723a 24f]).

68 Reproduced by Paré, G, 403; Rüff, G, 168; Mercuriale, IV.5, G, 273; Akakia, II.1, G, 774–7; de Castro, *De universa mulierum medicina*, I.45–8.

69 The bibliography of this debate is somewhat confused; it appears to begin with Mundinius's *Disputatio...de semine* (1609); followed by Liceti, *De perfecta constitutione hominis in utero* (1616); Parisano, *De subtilitate* (1621); Mundinius, *De genitura pro Galeno adversus peripateticos et nostrae aetatis philosophos et medicos disputatio* (1622); Parisano, *De semine a toto proventu* (1623); Mundinius, *Ad disputationem de Genitura additamentum apologeticum, in quo Aemilii Parisani opinionem de semine a toto proventu et de stygmatum causis ab omni probabilitate alienam esse sustinetur* (1625); Hofmann, *De generatione hominis contra Mundinum Mundinium* (1629); Cremonini, *De calido innato et semine, pro Aristotele adversus Galenum* (1634); Parisano, *De subtilitate pars altera* (1635).

70 Adelmann, *Marcello Malpighi*, II.760ff.

71 See Aristotle, *De generatione animalium*, IV.1 [765a 3ff].

72 e.g. Bonacciuoli, IV, G, 130; Levinus Lemnius, *Occulta naturae miracula* (1559), Antwerp, 1574, I.9, pp. 39–45.

73 The doubts, based on empirical evidence, are already voiced by Aristotle (*De generatione animalium*, IV.1 [765a 3ff]; see also Mercado, III.6, G, 1003–4. Another aspect of Pythagorean thought is found in the supposed relationship between length of pregnancy, survival of foetus and sex determination; see Mercado, IV.1, G, 1039–40, where the following diagram based on the association female–even, male–odd (see above, 1.1.3) promotes certain predictions:

74 See Pagel, *Das medizinische Weltbild des Paracelsus*, pp. 62–70.

75 *Occulta naturae miracula*, I.4, p. 15.

76 According to Platter, the virago does not menstruate, because she uses up her residues of fat and blood by a more active life (G, ✱✱✱2v). Dubois defines the virago as 'mulier barbata, vegeta, virilis, voce gravi, infoecunda, quia calor multus sanguinem dissipat' (G, 163). See also de Castro, *De universa mulierum medicina*, 1.96.

77 On preformation *versus* epigenesis, see J. Needham, *A history of embryology*, revised by A. Hughes, Cambridge, 1959, esp. pp. 115–78.

78 *Des monstres et prodiges*, ed. Céard, pp. 29–30.

79 *Observationes*, pp. 575–6, referred to as authoritative by de Castro, *De universa mulierum medicina*, I.11.

80 *De hermaphroditorum monstrosorumque partium natura* (1604), Oppenheim, 1614; also by Schenck von Grafenberg, *Observationes*, pp. 573–5.

81 See Mercado, III.7, G, 1005–12; Akakia, II.14, G, 793–4.

82 Although breasts are a secondary sexual characteristic considered at length in both anatomical and pathological studies, they are not of primary importance to the questions with which this study is concerned. They do, however, have a considerable metaphorical presence in iconology and in religious literature, representing humane or maternal feelings, nutritiousness and fecundity, and in iconography they are often the primary symbol of the difference of sex.

83 See Diepgen, in *Scientia*, LXXXIV, 132; Du Laurens, *Anatomica humani corporis historia*, VIII, q. 9, pp. 295–6. The *loci classici* are Aristotle, *Historia animalium*, III.19 [521a 22ff]; Pliny, *Natural history*, VII.15; Columella, *De re rustica*, XI.3, 31,50,64; Plutarch, *Symposium*, III, q. 4.

84 e.g. Dubois, G, 148; see also Tiraqueau, *De legibus connubialibus*, I.15.132, in *Opera omnia*, II.235; Nevizzano, *Sylva nuptialis*, p. 82.

85 Fernel, *Physiologia* (1554), VI.7, in *Universa medicina*, Hanau, 1610, pp. 166–8; Riolan, *Physiologia*, IV.8, in *Universae medicinae compendia*, Paris, 1598, fo. 33.

86 Bottoni, XIII, G, 347; Mercuriale, IV.1, G, 257–8; de Castro, *De universa mulierum medicina*, 1.78–80. See also Magirus, *Physiologia peripatetica*, V.15, p. 437; Du Laurens, *Anatomica humani corporis historia*, VIII, q. 8, pp. 294–5.

87 See Cardano, *De subtilitate*, XI, in *Opera omnia*, III.937; a *locus classicus* is Pliny, *Natural history*, XXVIII.6.18.

88 For a fuller account see Screech, *The Rabelaisian marriage*, pp. 84–103; R. Antonioli, *Rabelais et la médecine*, Geneva, 1976, (*Etudes Rabelaisiennes*, XII), pp. 195ff, esp. 198–9.

89 Bottoni, XXXIX, G, 368; Mercuriale, IV.20, G, 294; Akakia, 1.8, G, 760–3; Mercado, II.9, G, 929; de Castro, *De universa mulierum medicina*, 1.17–19. Fernel criticizes both Galen and Plato on this topic (*Pathologia*, VII.14, in *Universa medicina*, p. 327, referred to by La Corde, G, 545).

90 *De legibus connubialibus*, 1.9.92, in *Opera omnia*, II.143.

91 *Physiologia*, VII.5, in *Universae medicinae compendia*, fos. 73–4.

92 See G, 109.

93 One Aristotelian *locus* (*Historia animalium*, III.19 [521a 27]) suggests, however, that they are less prone to diseases of the blood.

94 See Mercado, 1.2, G, 807–8. The Hippocratic *locus* which attributes all female illnesses to the uterus is in *Places in men, ad. fin.* (see Hippocrates, *Opera omnia*, ed. A. Foesius, Geneva, 1657, p. 423), referred to by Du Laurens, *Anatomica humani corporis historia*, VII, q. 11, p. 277.

95 Mercado, II.10, G, 927; Cremonini, *Explanatio proemii librorum Aristotelis de physico auditu*, Padua, 1596, fo. 16v.

96 Mercado, II.10, G, 925–6; this state is most common in widows deprived of coitus, according to La Roche, V, G, 74. See also Galen, *De locis affectis*, VI.5.

97 II.4–10, G, 896ff.

98 The *locus classicus* is in Aristotle, *De partibus animalium*, II.7 (653b 1ff). See also Diepgen, in *Scientia*, LXXXIV, 55.

99 *Anatomica humani corporis historia*, VIII, q. 10, p. 297.

100 See Lemnius, *Occulta naturae miracula*, 1.4, pp. 15–16, and Mercado, III.7, G, 1011.

101 See Pagel, *Paracelsus: an introduction to philosophical medicine in the era of the Renaissance*, Basle and New York, 1958, p. 122.

102 With moist humours specifically, Scaliger associates changeability, lack of stamina and excessive delicacy ('fluxus; enervis; laboris impotens; deliciarum amator', *Exercitationes*, CCLXXIV).

103 For the presence of these ideas in popular literature, see Maclean, *Feminism in French literature*, pp. 46ff.

104 Cf. Seneca, *Epistolae*, XCV: 'pati natae'.

105 *De caussis pulsuum*, III.2.

106 I, G, 110.

107 Akakia, G, 745; de Castro, *De universa mulierum medicina*, 1.131. Du Laurens even accords them superior powers of mind ('memoria felicior, inventio subtilior, verborum quae animi conceptus experimunt copia maior', *Anatomica humani corporis historia*, VIII, q. 2, p. 282).

108 *Epistolae*, CXXII, PL, XII.1016: a Renaissance commonplace (see Caelius Rhodiginus, *Lectiones antiquae* (1517), Geneva, 1630, XIII.33, col. 718).

109 *Summa*, 1a 93,4.

110 *Adversaria seu commentarii medicinales*, Cologne, 1615, ¶3r–5r.

111 See Mercado, II.2, G, 882, where he claims that malfunction of the uterus can make women 'imbecilliores, ineptae ad actiones obeundas, tristes, taediosae'; and Mercuriale, 1.2, G, 213: 'passiones animi quod mirifice sterilitatem inducant, certum est: memini me legere apud quendam mulierem si in coitu ploret non posse concipere, sic etiam faciunt nimis timor, moeror et ira immodica'.

112 e.g. Plato, *Timaeus*, 91D; Aristotle, *De generatione animalium*, 1.2 [716a 15]; *Historia animalium*, VII.2 [582a 33]; Plutarch, *Symposium*, III, q. 4.

113 See R. Lenoble, *Mersenne ou la naissance du mécanisme*, Paris, 1943.

114 *Medicina universa*, p. 355. See also *Metaphysics*, Δ.4 [1014b 16ff].

115 See *Physics*, II.8–9 [198b 10ff], and *De generatione animalium*, V.1 [778a 29ff].

116 'Multa fiunt ex necessitate naturae, quae non fiunt ex eius intentione', quoted by Henning Arnisaeus (d. 1635), *De iure connubiorum*, Frankfurt, 1613, p. 150, attributed to *Physics*, II.9.
117 It was commonly believed after Aristotle that the normal lifespan of a woman was shorter than that of a man; the *locus classicus* is *Historia animalium*, VII.3 [583*b* 28].

CHAPTER 4

1 'Economic', when in inverted commas, is used here as the adjective of the practical philosophy of the household, not in its modern sense.
2 Evidence of use is found most frequently in the writings of clerics, e.g. Bartolomeo Spina (see Chap. 1, n.2) and Du Bosc, *La femme heroïque*, 1.8.
3 On the reception of this text, see J. Soudek, 'Leonardo Bruni and his public: a statistical and interpretative study of the annotated Latin version of the (Pseudo-) Aristotelian *Economics*', *Studies in medieval and Renaissance history*, V (1968), 51–136.
4 See *French moralists: the theory of the passions, 1585–1649*, Oxford, 1964.
5 *Statesman*, 258 Eff.
6 *Economics*, 1.1–2 [1252*a* 1ff]; Plutarch, *Septem sapientium convivium*, XII.
7 e.g. Vincent Cabot (fl. 1598–1620), *Les politiques*, Toulouse, 1630, 1.9, pp. 59–65.
8 e.g. Keckermann, *Synopsis disciplinae oeconomicae* (1607), Hanau, 1610, pp. 1–4.
9 Keckermann, *Systema ethicae* (1607), Hanau, 1610, pp. 10–13.
10 e.g. Hector Forestus, *In Ethica Aristotelis...domesticae praelectiones*, Lyons, 1550, pp. 241–2 (on whether it is better to go to the assistance of wife, child or father first, if all are in danger). Cf. in general Johannes Crellius (1590–1633), *Ethica aristotelica ad sacrarum literarum normam emendata* (1635).
11 Keckermann, *Systema ethicae*, p. 9; Guillaume Du Vair, *La philosophie morale des stoïques* (1585), III, in *Œuvres*, Rouen, 1636, p. 687.
12 Klemens Timpler (1562/3–1624), *Philosophiae practicae systema methodicum* (1608); *ethica*, Hanau, 1612, 1.3, p. 43.
13 Plato, *Timaeus*, 44Bff (in Timpler's interpretation); Aristotle, *Nicomachean Ethics*, VI.8 [1142*a* 11ff].
14 *Politics*, III.4 [1277*b* 25].
15 Niccolò Vito di Gozzi, *Dello stato delle republiche secondo la mente di Aristotele con essempli moderni*, Venice, 1591, p. 141; Antonio Montecatini (*c.* 1536–1599), *Politicorum...[liber] tertius Aristotelis conversus in Latinam linguam et commentariis illustratus*, Ferrara, 1597, p. 61.
16 There is a debate about the nature of slaves in mid-sixteenth-century Spain, largely connected with the status of Amerindians. For a full account, see the forthcoming study by A. Pagden, *The fall of natural man: the American Indian and the origins of historical relativism*, Cambridge, in preparation.
17 e.g. Gozzi, *Dello stato delle republiche*, p. 58; Montecatini, *In politica progymnasmata*, Ferrara, 1587, pp. 49–50; Cabot, *Les politiques*, pp. 106–7.
18 *In politica progymnasmata*, pp. 469–70, 483–4. But this resolution is not orthodox Aristotelianism; cf. *Politics*, 1.13, quoted in 4.4.3: 'all classes must be deemed to have their special attributes'.
19 e.g. by Forestus, *In Ethica Aristotelis*, p. 241; Gozzi, *Governo della famiglia*, Venice, 1589, p. 22.
20 See Timpler, *Philosophiae practicae systema: ethica*, II.5, p. 194; Crellius, *Ethica aristotelica*, Amsterdam, 1681, II.26, p. 191; Keckermann, *Systema ethicae*, p. 342.
21 The *locus classicus* is Lactantius, *De opificio Dei*, XII, who refers in turn to Varro.
22 Keckermann, *Systema ethicae*, pp. 309ff; Hubert van Giffen (Giphanius) (d. 1604), *Commentarii in decem libros Ethicorum Aristotelis ad Nicomachum* (1602), Frankfurt, 1608, pp. 325–9; Felice Figliucci (*c.* 1525–*c.* 1590), *De la filosofia morale libri dieci. Sopra li dieci libri de l' Ethica d' Aristotile*, Rome, 1551, pp. 180–2 (all by implication).
23 Epictetus, *Enchiridion*, LXII; Seneca, *Epistolae*, XCV.
24 *In libros politicos Aristotelis disputatio*, Venice, 1552, p. 175.
25 Keckermann, *Synopsis disciplinae oeconomicae*, p. 243 ('uxor voluntatem suam subiiciat voluntati et imperio mariti, atque in omnibus rebus honestis eius consilio obsequatur');

cf. Timpler, *Philosophiae practicae systema: oeconomia*, II.1, p. 130.

26 *De morali disciplina libri quinque*, Venice, 1552, III, p. 41.

27 *In politica progymnasmata*, pp. 469–73.

28 *Philosophiae practicae systema: ethica*, IV.1, p. 391 ('neque infantes, neque morones, neque deliri et amentes homines, quatenus sunt tales, actionum moralium sunt capaces'); cf. Montecatini, *In politica progymnasmata*, p. 473.

29 Cabot, *Les politiques*, pp. 105–6; Montecatini, *In politica progymnasmata*, pp. 483–4.

30 Theodor Zwinger, in *Aristotelis politicorum libri octo*, trans. Denis Lambin and Pier Vettori, Basle, 1582, p. 251. In another context, 'prudentia economica' could simply mean prudence applied to household matters by either men or women.

31 *De legibus connubialibus*, 1.1.89ff, in *Opera omnia*, II.19–20.

32 Cf. also Hippocrates, *Epidemics*, VI.4, quoted by Du Laurens, *Anatomica humani corporis historia*, VIII, q. 2, p. 284, and Seneca, *Controversiae*, II.7: 'muliebrium vitiorum fundamentum avaritia est', which contains a similar implication.

33 Cf. above, 2.12.2. For examples of the manipulation of ethical terms for artistic effect by trading upon these ambiguities, see Maclean, *Feminism in French literature*, pp. 249ff.

34 The *locus classicus* is Cicero, *Tusculanae disputationes*, II.18.

35 See Du Vair, *La philosophie morale des stoïques* (1585) and *De la constance et consolation ès calamités publiques* (1593); Justus Lipsius, *De constantia* (1584–5) and *Manuductio ad stoicam philosophiam* (1604). On neostoicism, in general, see L. Zanta, *La Renaissance du stoïcisme au XVIe siècle*, Paris, 1914.

36 For examples, see Maclean, *Feminism in French literature*, pp. 74ff.

37 Cf. Montaigne, *Essais*, ed. Thibaudet and Rat, II.17, p. 638.

38 *Colloquium abbatis et eruditae*, in *Opera omnia*, I.745.

39 It is interesting to align these reactions with N. Z. Davis's discussion of Alice Rossi's three models for talking about sex equality (*Society and culture in Early Modern France*, p. 93).

40 *Philosophiae practicae systema: ethica*, II.4, p. 169.

41 See Jacques Lefèvre d'Etaples (d. 1536), *Politicorum libri octo: commentarii* (1506), Paris, 1543, fo. 13v; Keckermann, *Synopsis disciplinae oeconomicae*, p. 9.

42 Arnisaeus, *Doctrina politica in genuinam methodum, quae est Aristotelis, reducta*, Frankfurt, 1606, pp. 56ff; Montecatini, *In politica progymnasmata*, pp. 17ff; Timpler, *Philosophiae practicae systema: oeconomia*, I.4, pp. 33–6. It is true to say, however, that these discussions all end with a condemnation of polygamy. See Chap. 4, n.85.

43 The allegorical sense of marriage is the union of Christ with the Church (Eph. 5:23); the anagogical sense is the union of humanity with the Word. See also Pierre de la Primaudaye (1546–1619), *Académie française*, Paris, 1581–96, I.144–58.

44 For the use of these arguments and of the double comparative, see Gozzi, *Dello stato delle republiche*, p. 141; Zwinger, in *Aristotelis politicorum libri octo*, trans. Lambin and Vettori, p. 251; Keckermann, *Synopsis disciplinae oeconomicae*, p. 12; Jean Crassot (c. 1558–1616), *La science morale d'Aristote*, Paris, 1617, p. 166; Crellius, *Ethica aristotelica*, II.24, p. 179. van Giffen gives contrary examples, but points out that these would be unnatural in Aristotle's eyes (*Commentarii in politicorum opus Aristotelis*, Frankfurt, 1608, p. 128).

45 See above, 2.9.1.

46 See Maclean, *Feminism in French literature*, pp. 228–9.

47 *Aristotelis de Republica libri octo*, Paris, 1548, fo. 26. Timpler refers to Plutarch's aphorism in the *Conjugalia praecepta* (VI) about the foolishness of wives who wish to dominate their husbands (*Philosophiae practicae systema: oeconomia*, II.1, p. 130).

48 *Corona virtutum moralium, universam Aristotelis ethicen exacte enucleans*, Frankfurt, 1601, VIII.10, p. 795.

49 Pier Vettori (1499–1585), in *Aristotelis politicorum libri octo*, trans. Lambin and Vettori, p. 97; Montecatini, *In politica progymnasmata*, pp. 26ff; Keckermann, *Synopsis disciplinae oeconomicae*, p. 20; Cabot, *Les politiques*, pp. 102–7.

50 Rafaele Maffei (Volaterranus) (1451–1521), *In Aristotelis Ethicam argumenta*, Venice, 1542, fo. 3r; Figliucci, *De la filosofia morale*, pp. 376–82; Keckermann, *Synopsis disciplinae oeconomicae*, pp. 15–16; van Giffen, *Commentarii in Ethica*, p. 680; Crassot, *La science morale*, p. 170.

51 See Zwinger, in *Aristotelis politicorum libri octo*, trans. Lambin and Vettori, p. 102.
52 Gozzi, *Governo della famiglia*, pp. 48–9; Vettori, in *Aristotelis politicorum libri octo*, trans. Lambin and Vettori, pp. 97ff; Keckermann, *Synopsis disciplinae oeconomicae*, pp. 24–8; Timpler, *Philosophiae practicae systema: oeconomia*, II.3, pp. 158–9; Cabot, *Les politiques*, pp. 101–14.
53 For exhaustive treatment of this topic, see Kelso, *Doctrine for the lady of the Renaissance*, Illinois, 1956. See also above, 3.9.1.
54 *Thesaurus oeconomiae, seu commentarius in Oeconomica Aristotelis*, Oxford, 1597, I.2, p. 29–30, quoted by Keckermann, *Synopsis disciplinae oeconomicae*, p. 4.
55 e.g. Vettori, in *Aristotelis politicorum libri octo*, trans. Lambin and Vettori, p. 11.
56 e.g. Montaigne, *Essais*, ed. Thibaudet and Rat, I.28, p. 185.
57 Classical models of the good wife frequently cited are Penelope and Alcestis (see Agostino Nifo (1473–1538), *Opuscula moralia et politica*, Paris, 1645, II.142; Gozzi, *Governo della famiglia*, p. 49).
58 Timpler, *Philosophiae practicae systema: oeconomia*, II.1, p. 130; Arnisaeus, *Doctrina politica*, p. 84.
59 Keckermann, *Synopsis disciplinae oeconomicae*, p. 30.
60 *De institutione foeminae Christianae*, T4vff; see also Keckermann, *Synopsis disciplinae oeconomicae*, p. 45.
61 e.g. Montaigne, *Essais*, ed. Thibaudet and Rat, II.8, p. 376.
62 The Platonic *loci* most frequently referred to are *Republic*, V; *Laws*, VII; *Meno*, 72Aff. Plutarch's *Mulierum virtutes* is also much quoted.
63 In Plutarch's Life of Lycurgus (XIV) there is a defence of Lycurgus against Aristotle; Renaissance commentators sometimes cite this (e.g. Lefèvre d'Etaples, *Politicorum libri octo: commentarii*, fo. 33r).
64 See Caelius Rhodiginus, *Lectiones antiquae*, XIV.14, col. 756.
65 Filippo de Franchi (Francus) (fl. 1499), in *Commentarii ad titulum Digestorum de regulis antiqui*, Lyons, 1593, p. 51.
66 e.g. Jean Bodin (1530–96), *Les six livres de la république* (1576), Paris, 1580, VI.5, pp. 1001–13; Pierre Grégoire (c. 1540–97), *De republica*, Frankfurt, 1597, pp. 443–79; Keckermann, *Systema disciplinae politicae* (1607), Hanau, 1608, pp. 40–3; Giovanni Stefano Menochi (d. 1656), *Institutiones politicae e sacris scripturis depromptae*, Lyons, 1625, pp. 63–73. Justus Lipsius is equivocal on this point; he thinks women are capable of ruling, but should not do so if this infringes 'lex aut mos' (*Politica*, II.3, in *Opera omnia*, Lyons, 1613, II.52).
67 For a summary bibliography of polemical writings against these queens, many of them connected with the debate about Salic Law, see Maclean, *Feminism in French literature*, p. 58, and below, 5.3.3.
68 e.g. Cabot, *Les politiques*, pp. 111–13.
69 *Sphaera civitatis*, Oxford, 1588, I.3, pp. 32–3, 40–1.
70 e.g. Timpler, *Philosophiae practicae systema: politica*, IV.10, pp. 496–7.
71 *De his quae ab optimis principibus agenda sunt*, in *Opuscula moralia et politica*, II.139–48.
72 Cf. Zwinger, who extrapolates the text of *Politics*, III.4 (1277b 20) by adding 'vir timidus iudicabitur, si ita fortis ut mulier. Mulier econtra audax, si virilem fortitudinem exprimat' (in *Aristotelis politicorum libri octo*, trans. Lambin and Vettori, p. 251).
73 *Della virtù feminile e donnesca*, in *Le prose diverse*, ed. C. Guasti, Florence, 1875, II.203ff. Refuted by Lucrezia Marinella, *La nobiltà et l'eccellenza delle donne* (1600), Venice, 1621, pp. 171–4; Pierre Le Moyne, *Gallerie des femmes fortes*, Paris, 1647, p. 172. A similar division of nature and convention (φυσις and νομος) is an important theme also in Tasso's pastoral drama *L'Aminta* (1573).
74 For examples, see Maclean, *Feminism in French literature*, pp. 83ff, 229n.
75 One may note with interest that commentators on *Politics*, V.11 [1313b 30ff] neglect in the main to develop this potential *locus classicus* on the association of women and political intrigue. One rare example of comment is by Vettori, in *Aristotelis politicorum libri octo*, trans. Lambin and Vettori, p. 463.
76 e.g. by Montaigne, *Essais*, ed. Thibaudet and Rat, I.56, p. 310. See also N. Z. Davis, *Society and culture in Early Modern France*, pp. 77ff.

77 See Aquinas, *Summa*, 2a 2ae 82,3.

78 See Agrippa d'Aubigné (1551?–1630), *Œuvres*, ed. E. Réaume and F. de Caussade, Paris, 1873–7, I.445.

79 On this topic, see M. A. Screech, 'La querelle des amyes', *Bibliothèque d'humanisme et Renaissance*, XXI (1959), 103–30.

80 See Kelso, *Doctrine for the lady of the Renaissance*, pp. 58–77.

81 See Maclean, *Feminism in French literature*, pp. 135ff.

82 See *In politica progymnasmata*, pp. 483–4. Montecatini also wrote a commentary on Plato's *Republic* (1594).

83 e.g. Antoine Hotman, *Observationum quae ad veteres nuptiarum ritum pertinent liber singularis* (1585); Cholières, *La forêt nuptiale, où est représentée une variété bigarrée. . .de divers mariages selon qu'ils sont observés et pratiqués par plusieurs peuples et nations étranges* (1600).

84 *Essais*, ed. Thibaudet and Rat, III.5, pp. 818–76.

85 On Milton, see J. Cairncross, *After polygamy was made a sin*, London, 1974, pp. 126–38; de Pure, *La prétieuse* (1656–8), ed. E. Magne, Paris, 1938–9, II.18ff; on earlier discussion of polygamy, notably by Bernardino Ochino (*Dialogus de polygamia* (1563)), see Cairncross, *Polygamy*, pp. 65–73.

86 See L. M. Richardson, *The forerunners of feminism in the French literature of the Renaissance*, Baltimore, London and Paris, 1929, pp. 73ff, 110ff; C. Camden, *The Elizabethan woman*, New York and London, 1952, pp. 239–71; Kelso, *Doctrine for the lady of the Renaissance*, pp. 58–77.

CHAPTER 5

1 *La Femme* (recueils de la société Jean Bodin pour l'histoire comparative des institutions, XI–XII), Brussels, 1959–62.

2 See D. R. Kelley, *Foundations of modern historical scholarship: language, law and history in the French Renaissance*, New York and London, 1970.

3 On the meaning of *res*, see Kelley, *Foundations*, pp. 29, 130.

4 e.g. by Conrad Haas (Lagus) (d. 1546?), *Methodica iuris utriusque traditio* (1545), Lyons, 1566, pp. 70–2, and *passim*.

5 *De verborum significatione libri quatuor. . .* (1529), Frankfurt, 1582, esp. pp. 204–9; see also Kelley, *Foundations*, pp. 91–101.

6 On this topic, see L. J. Cohen, *The diversity of meaning*, pp. 5ff.

7 Alciato, *De verborum significatione*, CXXXV, pp. 458–60; Tiraqueau, *De legibus connubialibus*, I.1.69, I.9.228, in *Opera omnia*, II.15, 170.

8 *Observationes et emendationes*, VI.21, in *Opera omnia*, Lyons, 1606, IV.1484.

9 *Parerga*, Frankfurt, 1588, I.3, pp. 9–11.

10 *De origine idololatriae*, III.48, in *Opera omnia*, V.361–2.

11 See Wolff, *Discursus*, H2r–v; Eberartus, *Bonus mulier*, E3v–4v.

12 e.g. Wolff; Eberartus; Hieronymus Treutler (1566?–1607), *Selectae disputationes ad jus civile* (1597), Marburg, 1603, I.18–19; Johannes Harpprecht (1560–1639), *Tractatus criminalis*, Frankfurt, 1603, p. 381.

13 *Commentarius repetitae praelectionis in tit. xvi lib. 1 Pandectarum*, Nassau, 1614, p. 34: 'plus aut minus nulli rei specificam tribuat differentiam, sive formam, quantitate vel qualitate subjectum tantummodo distinguens'.

14 *Ibid.* pp. 35–7. A subsequent legal disputation on the same topic between Franz Hoeltich and Johannes Waltz is published at Wittenberg in 1672, entitled *Quaestio foemina non est homo*.

15 *Bonus mulier*, E3v–E4r.

16 See above, 4.4.2, and Tiraqueau, *De legibus connubialibus*, I.1.55, in *Opera omnia*, II.12; Anon., *The lawes resolutions of women's rights: or the lawes provision for women*, London, 1632, p. 4.

17 See Pontus de Tyard, *De recta nominum impositione*, Lyons, 1603, for an example of Renaissance cratylism, and G. Genette, *Mimologiques: voyage en Cratylie*, Paris, 1976.

18 See Valla, *Elegantiae*, VI.38, cited by Kelley, *Foundations*, p. 42; Alciato, *De verborum significatione*, XIII, p. 233.

19 *The lawes resolutions of women's rights*, p. 2.

20 See Goeddeus, *Commentarius in tit. xvi lib. 1 Pandectarum*, p. 38.

21 See Gratian, *Decretum*, XXXIII.5; Tiraqueau, *De legibus connubialibus*, 1.15.126–36, in *Opera omnia*, II.234–6; and R. Metz, 'Le statut de la femme en droit canonique médiéval', in *La Femme*, II.59–113.

22 For a comprehensive list of references to these characteristics in women in Civil and Canon Law, see Tiraqueau, *De legibus connubialibus*, 1.1.70–6, in *Opera omnia*, II.16–18.

23 *The lawes resolutions of women's rights*, p. 5.

24 See Gregorius Rolbag, *Certamen masculo-foemineum super aequitate, utilitate et necessitate differentiarum sexus in successionibus*, Speyer, 1602, pp. 394–5.

25 *Ad leges de iure civile Voconiam, Falcidiam, Juliam Papiam Poppaeam, Rhodiam, Aquilam*, Basle, 1559. See also *Codex*, 6.28.4, and Cabot, *Variarum iuris publici et privati disputationes*, Paris, 1598, 1.19.

26 *Foundations*, pp. 199ff.

27 *Praxis civilis ex antiquis et recentioribus authoribus Germanis, Italis, Gallis, Hispanis, Belgis et aliis*, Frankfurt, 1591, 1.296–7.

28 *In sextum Codicis librum praelectiones*, ed. Philippus Decius, Lyons, 1545, fo. 165v (on *Codex*, 6.55.12).

29 See the *Tractatus iuris universi*, Venice, 1584, X.2, 165–71. For a later conservative view, see Johannes Wenemar Konig, *Disputatio inauguralis de differentiis utriusque sexus in iure*, Strasbourg, 1662, pp. 21ff.

30 The title of the 1606 edition is *Responsum juris, an foeminae, ab eisque descendentes in successionibus regnorum, ducatuum, comitatuum etc. ab intestato venientium, extantibus masculis, jure excludantur.*

31 *Ingolstadiensis Academiae consilia in causa successionis inter Dominum Baronem de Sprinzenstein et Dominum de Rechenberger*, Ingolstadt, 1614; *Rostochiensium jurisconsultorum responsa ad Ingolstadiensis Academiae consilia in causa Sprinzensteiniana*, Rostock, 1615; Matthaeus Polenius, *Defensio causae Sprinzensteinianae de privilegiis foeminae per masculos excludentibus*, Frankfurt, 1614; *idem*, *Antapologia pro defensione causae Sprinzensteinianae*, Frankfurt, 1615; Anon., *Deductio in jure et facto Henrici Melchioris von Rechenberger contra Hans Ernsten Sprinzenstein*, Frankfurt, 1615; *Ingolstadiensis Academiae responsum in causa Sprinzensteiniana*, Ingolstadt, 1616. I have been unable to locate these works; they are cited in Martin Lipenius, *Bibliotheca realis juridica*, Frankfurt, 1679, pp. 196, 499. See also Albertus Brunus, *Commentarii super statutis excludentibus foeminas et cognatorum lineam a successionibus*, in *Tractatus de statutis*, Frankfurt, 1606, pp. 334–643; Gothofredus Antonius (1571–1618), *Disputatio de foeminarum in feudis successione et exclusione*, Giessen, 1607 (cited by Lipenius, *Bibliotheca realis juridica*, p. 196).

32 Gaudentius (d. 1649), *Dissertatio de successione foeminarum*, Strasbourg, 1654; Herzholm, *Diatribe in exercitationem Paganini Gaudentii de successione foeminarum*, Copenhagen, 1663 (cited by Lipenius, *Bibliotheca realis juridica*, p. 196).

33 *Relectiones*, Salamanca, 1565, fos. 60–2; d'Alvin, *Tractatus*, fos. 1–20. See also R. Metz, 'Le statut de la femme en droit canonique médiéval', in *La Femme*, II.99.

34 *The lawes resolutions of women's rights*, p. 6.

35 *De legibus connubialibus*, in *Opera omnia*, II.1ff (Coutume de Poitou, XV: 'de la puissance et administration des marys').

36 For an extensive discussion of divorce and polygamy, see Henning Arnisaeus, *De iure connubiorum*, Frankfurt, 1613, IV, pp. 253–91, VI, pp. 259–336 (=359–436).

37 See *ibid*. p. 361 (=461), where there is a bibliography of Renaissance texts on this topic, and *The lawes resolutions of women's rights*, pp. 128–9.

38 *Ibid*. p. 4.

39 See Barthélemy de Chasseneuz (d. 1542), *Catalogus gloriae mundi* (1528), Lyons, 1546, fo. 58; Johannes Ferrarius, in *Commentarii de regulis juris antiqui*, p. 49.

40 'Foeminae ab omnibus officiis civilibus, vel publicis remotae sunt: et ideo nec judices esse possunt, nec magistratum gerere, nec postulare, nec pro alio intervenire, nec procuratores existere'. 'Judices': those who decided on the facts of a civil or criminal case; people on the *album judicum* (see W. W. Buckland, *A textbook of Roman Law*, 2nd edn, Cambridge, 1950, pp. 635ff).

41 Earlier editions of the commentaries of Francus, Decius, Ferrarius, Cagnoli and Raevardus appear in 1499, 1525, 1546, 1576 and 1568, respectively.

42 See Francus, in *Commentarii de regulis juris antiqui*, p. 57.

43 For Sparta, see above, 4.6.1; ancient Gaul and the Celtic tribes are especially noted by French writers (e.g. Lefèvre d'Etaples, *Politicorum libri octo: commentarii*, fo. 32v; Cabot, *Les politiques*, pp. 104–5). The historical source is Caesar, *De bello gallico*, VI).

44 See Francus, in *Commentarii de regulis juris antiqui*, p. 53.

45 e.g. Keckermann, *Systema disciplinae politicae*, pp. 40–3; Hieronymus Höfflich, *De foeminis ad officia publica non recipiendis*, Altdorf, 1620, Clr.

46 e.g. Francus, in *Commentarii de regulis juris antiqui*, p. 52.

47 A comprehensive list of occurrences of these words in Roman Law may be found in Tiraqueau, *De legibus connubialibus*, 1.1.70–6, in *Opera omnia*, II.15–17.

48 *Ibid.* 1.9.43ff, in *Opera omnia*, II.134–42.

49 Late Renaissance jurists make reference to medieval glosses on the *De quaestionibus* (*Digest*, 48.18.18) by Guido de Suzaria (*Tractatus de tormentis*, in *Tractatus de iudiciis et tortura*, ed. Francesco Bruni, Lyons, 1547, p. 175), Baldus (*Tractatus de quaestionibus et tormentis, ibid.* p. 229), and Alberto de Gandino (*Tractatus de maleficiis*, in *De maleficiis tractatus*, ed. Angelo Gambiglione, Venice, 1598, fo. 306): see Wolff, *Discursus*, H2, and Benedictus Carpzov (1595–1666), *Centuria positionum juridicarum de juribus foeminarum singularibus*, Leipzig, 1651, X.1.41ff.

50 For supporting texts from Roman Law, see Godefroy, *Praxis civilis*, p. 290.

51 See *The lawes resolutions of women's rights*, p. 2.

52 On these prerogatives, see Decius, in *Commentarii de regulis juris antiqui*, pp. 37ff, and Godefroy, *Praxis civilis*, pp. 291–3. A frequently cited work which I was unable to locate is by Friedrich Prückmann (1572–1630), *Repetitiones L. in multis ff. de statu hominis* (= *Digest*, 1.5.9, 'in multis juris nostri articulis deterior est conditio foeminarum quam masculorum'), Frankfurt, 1586.

53 See F. Joüon des Longrais, 'Le statut de la femme en Angleterre dans le droit commun médiéval', in *La Femme*, II.243–4.

54 *Discursus*, H2. Some lawyers even comment on medical issues concerning woman, such as the 'sutura saggitalis'; see Arnisaeus, *De iure connubiorum*, 1, p. 13, and above, 3.7.4.

55 See Joüon des Langrais, 'Le statut de la femme en Angleterre', in *La Femme*, II.235–41. But some theoretical writings still contain justifications of the *deterior conditio*: see Höfflich, *De foeminis ad officia publica non recipiendis*, and Everardus Bronchorst (1554–1627), *In tit. Digestorum de diversis regulis juris antiqui enarrationes* (1607), Leyden, 1648, pp. 6–7.

56 *De nobilitate et praecellentia foeminei sexus...declamatio*, Antwerp, 1529, C7.

57 *The lawes resolutions of women's rights*, pp. 2, 6.

CHAPTER 6

1 'Tout auteur a un sens auquel tous les passages contraires s'accordent, ou il n'a point de sens du tout', *Pensées*, 257, in *Œuvres complètes*, ed. L. Lafuma, Paris, 1972, p. 533.

2 *De iis quae scripta sunt physicè in sacris libris*; *Colloquia physica*; cf. also Menochi, *Institutiones politicae e sacris Literis depromptae*; Crellius, *Ethica aristotelica ad sacrarum Literarum normam emendata*; Zacchias, *Quaestiones medicolegales*.

3 Interdisciplinarity is argued here to be an agent of stasis; in other contexts, it may be seen to be the catalyst of scientific advance. Cf. A. Koestler, *The act of creation*, New York, 1964, p. 230, quoted by Kelley, *Foundations*, p. 9.

4 Respectively *Dies geniales* (1522); *De honesta disciplina* (1500); *Officina* (1520); *Lectiones antiquae* (1517).

5 *Utopia*, in *Complete works*, ed. E. Surtz and J. H. Hexter, New Haven and London, 1965, IV.190; *Gargantua*, ch. 57, in *Œuvres complètes*, ed. J. Boulenger and L. Scheler, Paris, 1965, p. 160.

6 'Je sçay mieux que c'est homme que je ne sçay que c'est animal, ou mortel, ou raisonnable', *Essais*, ed. Thibaudet and Rat, III.13, p. 1046.

7 'Verba significant, et res significantur. Et est significare, demonstrare rem de qua quaeritur, proprio nomine et attributo'.

8 Augustine, *City of God*, XXI.8, *PL*, XLI.721–2, quoted and elucidated by Montaigne, *Essais*, ed. Thibaudet and Rat, III.13, p. 1047.
9 See H. J. Eysenck, *The psychology of politics*, London, 1954, pp. 107ff, esp. 199ff.
10 On this topic, see Carl Degler, *Is there a history of women?*, Oxford, 1975, pp. 6–7.
11 For an example of one society, see C. Lougee, *Le paradis des femmes: women, salons, and social stratification in seventeenth-century France*, Princeton, 1976, esp. pp. 113–70.
12 See Kelso, *Doctrine for the lady of the Renaissance*.
13 See N. Z. Davis, *Society and culture in Early Modern France*, pp. 65–95; K. V. Thomas, 'Women and the Civil War Sects', *Past and present*, XIII, 42–62.
14 See H. Trevor-Roper, *The European witch-craze*, Harmondsworth, 1969; K. V. Thomas, *Religion and the decline of magic*, London, 1971.
15 See *Not in God's image*, ed. Julia O'Faolain and Lauro Martines, London, 1973, pp. 207–17, for illustrative texts.
16 See H. Marracci, *Biblioteca mariana*, 2 vols., Rome, 1648 for bibliographical evidence, and C. Flachaire, *La dévotion à la Vierge dans la littérature catholique au commencement du XVIIe siècle*, Paris, 1916.
17 On baroque artists, see Maclean, *Feminism in French literature*, pp. 212ff; on active versus passive portrayal, see John Berger, *Ways of seeing*, Harmondsworth, 1972, pp. 45ff.
18 See *Apologia adversus calumnias, propter declamationem de vanitate scientiarum*, XLII, quoted by M. A. Screech, 'Rabelais, de Billon and Erasmus', *Bibliothèque d'humanisme et Renaissance*, XIII (1951), 246.
19 See M. Angenot, *Les champions des femmes: examen du discours sur la supériorité des femmes, 1400–1800*, Montréal, 1977, pp. 151ff.
20 On these models, see Chap. 4, n.39.
21 For the bibliography of these debates, see Kelso, *Doctrine for the lady of the Renaissance*; Camden, *The Elizabethan woman*; Maclean, *Feminism in French literature*; Conor Fahy, 'Three Early Renaissance treatises on women', *Italian studies*, XI (1959), 30–55.
22 *Dialogue concerning the two chief world systems*, trans. Stillman Drake, Berkeley and Los Angeles, 1953, pp. 56–7.

Index